STEPHEN BALDWIN

livin it
TESTIMONIES

NASHVILLE, TENNESSEE

Livin It: Testimonies
Copyright © 2006 by Luis Palau Evangelistic Association
All Rights Reserved
Printed in the USA

ISBN 0-8054-4346-0
ISBN 13: 978-0-8054-4346-2
B & H Publishing Group
Nashville, Tennessee

Art Direction by Jeff Godby
Cover Design by Blake Morgan
Interior Design by Roy Roper, wideyedesign

Unless otherwise noted, all Scripture quotations have been
taken from the Holman Christian Standard Bible®
Copyright © 1999, 2000, 2002, 2003 by Holman Bible Publishers.

Dewey Decimal Classification: 248.83
Subject Heading: CHRISTIAN LIFE

1 2 3 4   09 08 07 06

WE ARE NOT RELIGIOUS....
WE ARE FOLLOWERS OF JESUS CHRIST
EVERYTHING WE ARE
AND EVERYTHING WE HAVE,
HOLDS NO TITLES.

UNTITLED SKATEBOARDS
FOR MORE INFO EMAIL US AT
INFO@UNTITLEDSKATEBOARDS.COM

9 For if you confess with your mouth that Jesus is Lord and believe in your heart that God raised him from the dead, you will be saved,

10 For it is by believing in your heart that you are made right with God, and it is by confessing with your mouth that you are saved.

ROMANS 10:9-10

LEFT TO RIGHT:
DAVE NELSON, SHAWN HALE,
NATHAN GIARRATANO, JARED LEE,
JAY ALABAMY HAIZLIP, JUD FARMBOY HEALD

untitled
skateboards

AVAILABLE FOR BOOKING
BOOKING@UNTITLEDSKATEBOARDS.COM

Therefore they spent a long time there speaking boldly with RELIANCE upon the Lord, who was testifying to the word of His grace, granting that signs and wonders be done by their hands.
Acts 14:3

Elijah Moore

Elijah Moore
PRO MODELS OUT NOW!

www.RELIANCESKATE.com
DEALER INQUIRES CALL 208-466-3968

LUKE BRADDOCK • TIM BYRNE • MASON CORNWELL • RICHARD JEFFERSON
JOSHUA KASPER • URIEL LUEBCKE • ELIJAH MOORE
AMS: ZAC ARCHULETA • MIKE BALD • COREY DENOMY • JOSE SANDOVAL
DAVE VOETBERG • CHRIS WEIGELE • CASEY WELLS

CONTENTS

INTRODUCTION
1-4

1 CHRISTIAN HOSOI
5-14

2 TIM BYRNE
15-24

3 ANTHONY CARNEY
25-34

4 SIERRA FELLERS
35-44

5 BRUCE CRISMAN
45-52

6 ELIJAH MOORE
53-62

7 JARED LEE
63-72

8 PHIL TROTTER
73-80

9 JOSH KASPER
81-90

10 JEREMIAH ANDERSON
91-98

11 CHRIS WEIGELE
99-108

12 VIC MURPHY
109-118

13 BRAD COLEMAN
119-126

14 LUKE BRADDOCK
127-136

RU LIVIN IT?
137

INTRODU

TELL YOU SOMETHIN'...

NOT LONG AFTER OUR WEDDING, MY WIFE, KENNYA, AND I MOVED DOWN TO ARIZONA, WHERE I WAS DOING A TV SHOW CALLED "THE YOUNG RIDERS."

It was my first big acting job, and they were going to pay me a lot of money every week. I was going to make more money each month than my dad made his entire school year as a teacher in New York. During that time, Kennya decided to hire a Brazilian lady—Augusta—to come help her around the house. When Augusta arrived, she didn't speak any English, only Portuguese with my wife. But on her very first day, Augusta started singing about Jesus Christ. / When my wife asked her about the singing, Augusta began to laugh. This made my wife raise her eyebrows and ask, "What's so funny?"

introduction 1

"I didn't mean any disrespect," she replied. "I just find it so funny that you think I am here to work for you and clean your house, because what I know is I have been sent here to bring you and your husband to Jesus Christ."

So my wife came and knocked on the door to my office.

"Honey, guess what Augusta said? She says she's here because someday **WE'RE GOING TO BECOME BORN-AGAIN CHRISTIANS.** Guess who started laughing then?

Well, to make a long story short, a few years later my wife really did come to faith in Jesus Christ—in 2000. She had been attending a very, very evangelical Brazilian church in New York, and after attending this church for two years, she became a born-again Christian.

For the next year, I watched my wife of ten years, my best friend, develop a powerful relationship with Jesus. I've been around the world. I've seen things, been places, hung out with movie stars, and made millions and millions of dollars. But nothing could compare to the experience of watching my wife grow into her newfound faith in Jesus Christ.

One day, Kennya came to me and said, "I really believe that we're going to be together forever, Stephen. But I want you to know that I'm going to follow Jesus Christ. And if you don't, then I can't promise that we're going to be together."

That conversation was definitely not easy for me, and I know it was even harder for Kennya. But it was the turning point for me. Not long after that conversation, I also surrendered my life to Jesus.

I'd have to say, though, that another big influence on my decision to accept Jesus Christ as Savior were the 9/11 attacks. That day changed my life forever, because it was an event that I had thought was a total impossibility. I could never believe that something like that could happen. But it did.

So after that national tragedy, and after my wife's conversion, I came to understand something. The impossible was possible. For Kennya, for America, even for me. And if anything's possible, then Jesus Christ could come back to this planet tomorrow, just like he said.

A couple years after I became a Christian, I was at a Luis Palau Festival in Fort Lauderdale, Florida, and I saw them using skateboarding to reach out to the kids. Growing up on Long Island, New York, I lived to skateboard. I was just a little punk amateur guy, denting people's cars and getting into trouble. But how my life would have been different as a kid if a skateboarder I looked up to had shared the good news with me!

That thought led me to an amazing ministry idea—to produce a DVD featuring skateboarders who live for Jesus Christ! So I pitched my idea to Luis Palau's team. And ever since I made that pitch, the Lord has been turning my idea into a reality. People started coming out of the woodwork, offering their skills and gifts to make the DVD happen.

The video I produced with the Palau organization is called Livin It. We distributed 100,000 of these DVDs in the first 18 months. It was an unbelievably awesome situation! And the sequel, Livin It LA, is just as awesome!

After that, we created a skateboarding tour, the Livin It Skate Tour, which has now become the ministry I work with all the time.

I've been very blessed in my life. But nothing has brought me more excitement and satisfaction than living for Jesus Christ. You, too, can have the amazing experience of following Jesus, the one and only true way to God. He's already reaching out to you. I mean, look—you're reading about him right now, aren't you? But the only way you can come into this experience is if you become willing to take the next step.

You can't understand what the Bible teaches until you have the Spirit of God in your life. And you can't have the Spirit of God in your life until you let him in . . . by faith.

Hebrews 11 explains that faith is being confident and assured of what you hope for—even though you can't see it! It's a blind first step. But once you take it, God sends his Spirit into your life and you come into the understanding. Trust me. I know. It's happened to me. And now all I want to do is live for Jesus.

As you flip through these pages, you will meet fourteen amazing guys. Some of them are skateboarders. Some are BMXers. Many of them were part of one of the Livin It DVDs. Others are part of the Livin It Tour. Some are still in their teens. A few have been skating or riding for more than 20 years. But they all have one thing in common—they are Livin It!

What does that mean? Basically, it means they've found a purpose in life that's way beyond this earth. A lot of them have tried to find happiness in money, fame, drugs, sex, partying, and other things, and been left unsatisfied. Only Jesus Christ could fill the void in their lives, and they want to share their stories with you.

READ ON TO FIND OUT HOW EXTREME ATHLETES FROM COAST TO COAST AND AROUND THE WORLD ARE

LIVIN IT FOR JESUS CHRIST!

STEPHEN BALDWIN

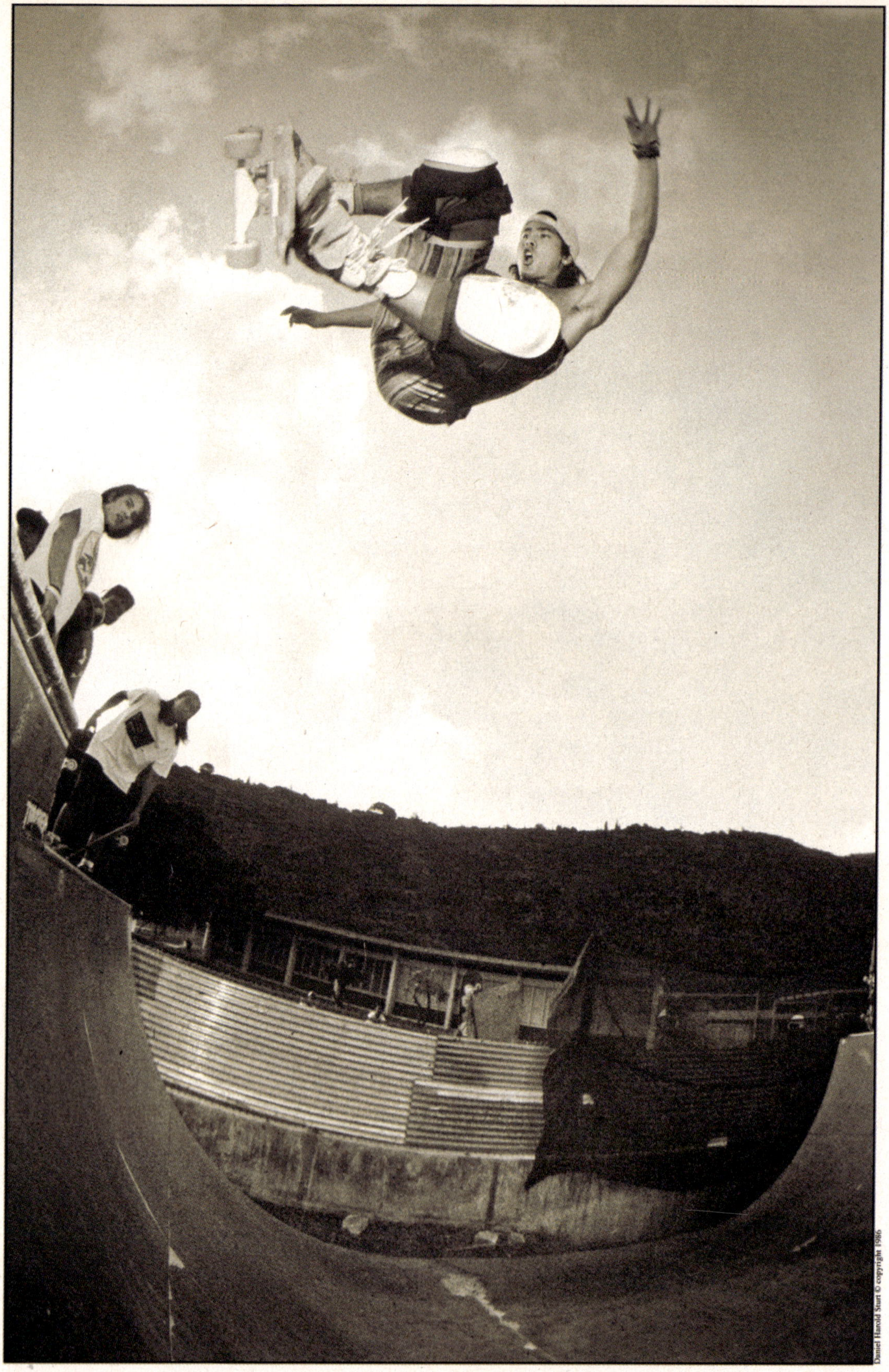

Tracker Trucks ~ Since 1975 ~ Quality Never Goes Out Of Style
Lester Kasai circa 1986 / www.trackertrucks.com

CHAPTER 1
CHRISTIAN HOSOI

CHRISTIAN HOSOI TURNED PROFESSIONAL AT 14, THEN NEARLY LOST EVERYTHING TO A DRUG ADDICTION. FIND OUT HOW THIS WORLD-RENOWNED SKATEBOARDER ROSE FROM ROCK BOTTOM TO FIND A FIRM FOUNDATION IN WHAT SEEMED LIKE THE MOST UNLIKELY PLACE.

THE IRON DOOR

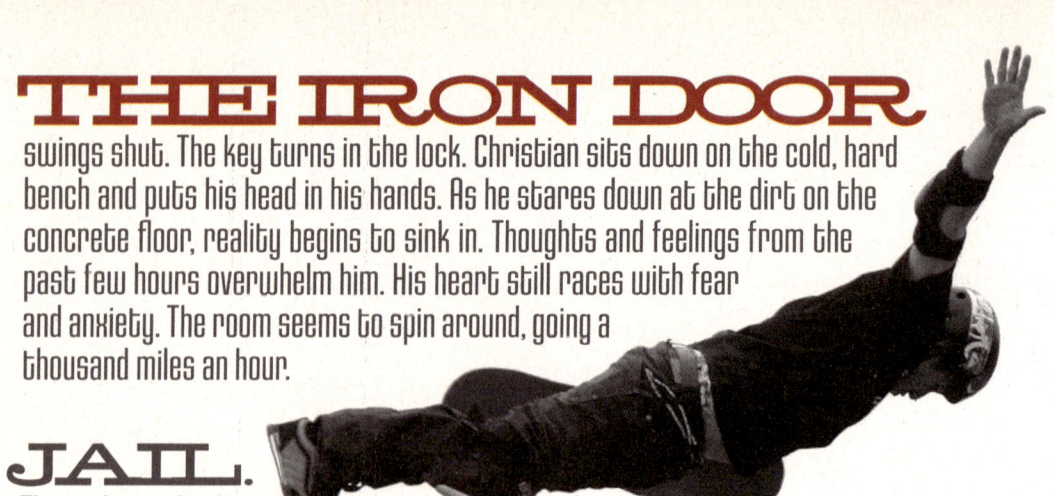

swings shut. The key turns in the lock. Christian sits down on the cold, hard bench and puts his head in his hands. As he stares down at the dirt on the concrete floor, reality begins to sink in. Thoughts and feelings from the past few hours overwhelm him. His heart still races with fear and anxiety. The room seems to spin around, going a thousand miles an hour.

JAIL.

The reality sinks deeper. Desperation and panic flood his mind. "I'm in jail, and I'm going to be in jail for a long time. **But wait a minute! I have friends. They'll bail me out. My lawyer can get me out of this!** Christian takes a deep breath. There's no use. He's out of excuses. He was caught red-handed. There's no way out. It would be hard to find a skateboarder who didn't know the name Christian Hosoi—a legend in the skating world. So how did this successful athlete end up behind bars? / "I could always get myself out of a situation, until I finally landed in prison," Christian says. "Sometimes we have to hit rock bottom before we say, 'Look, I can't get any further down than this.' I landed in prison because of drug addiction and putting my family last—even skateboarding last—and putting drugs and partying first." / Christian realized that his life had spiraled out of control. "There were no more strings. It was done. All the lines were cut. The key was thrown away. I said to myself, 'It's time to wake up, Christian. Face the music. This is serious. And it's real. And you're facing it. You're reaping what you sowed, and this is what you have to deal with.'"

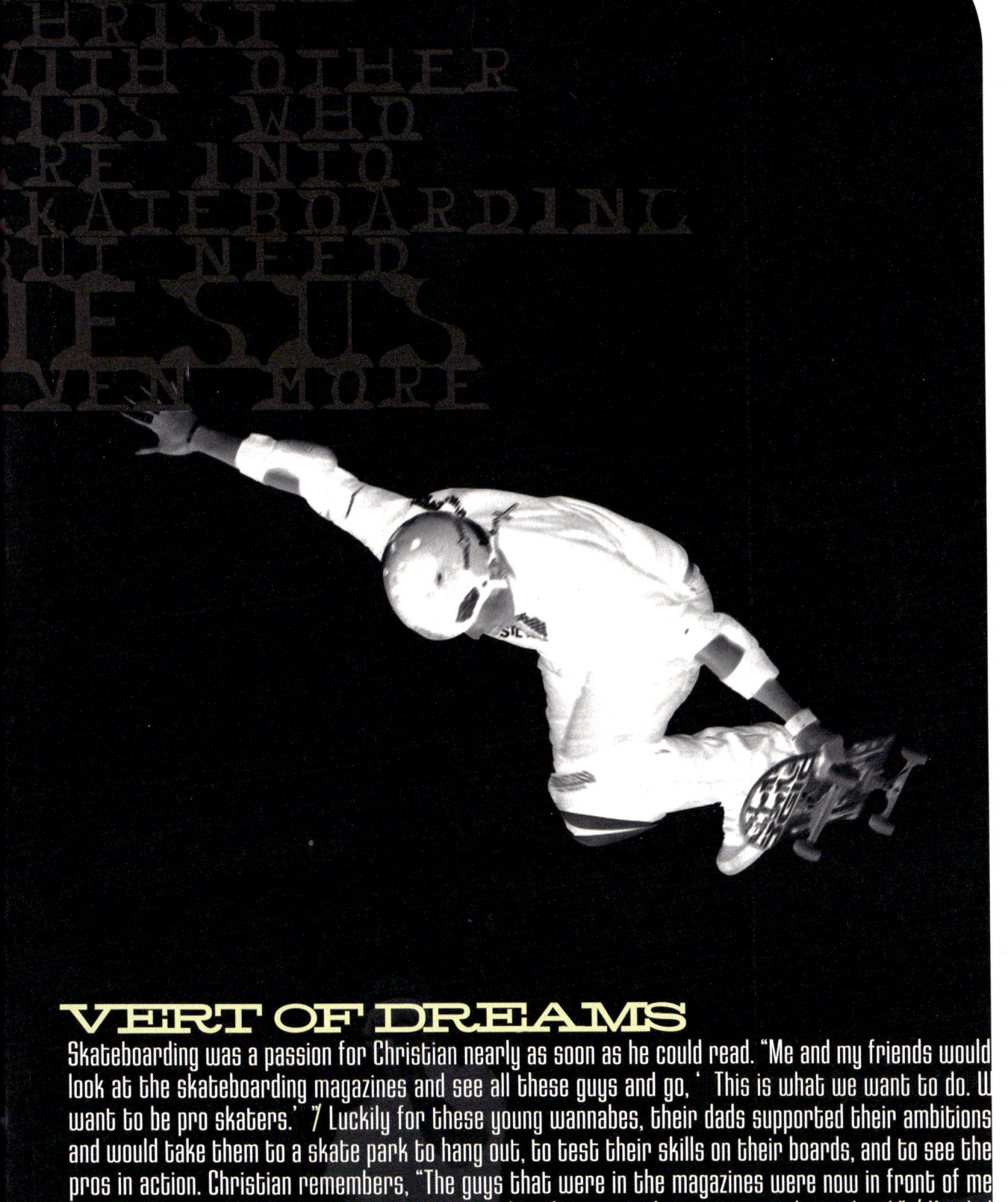

VERT OF DREAMS

Skateboarding was a passion for Christian nearly as soon as he could read. "Me and my friends would look at the skateboarding magazines and see all these guys and go, ' This is what we want to do. We want to be pro skaters.' / Luckily for these young wannabes, their dads supported their ambitions and would take them to a skate park to hang out, to test their skills on their boards, and to see the pros in action. Christian remembers, "The guys that were in the magazines were now in front of me live. We were so blown away that all we wanted to do was go there every single weekend." / His dad recognized Christian's natural talent and love for skateboarding, so he decided to apply to be manager of the skate park—and he landed the job. With his dad now in charge of the park, Christian could skate eight hours a day if he wanted. / "I ended up being friends with all my idols," he says. "The pros became like my big brothers, and I got good pretty much in a month's time or so."/ By the time he was 12, he was the top amateur in the nation. Two years later, he turned professional—and it didn't take long the name Christian Hosoi to rank among the top extreme sports athletes in the world.

8 Livin'It Testimonies

Christian had it made. By 17 he had a successful career, popularity, money, his own business, making over $250,000 a year—but none of it really made him happy.

So he decided to just "go have fun for a little while."

"That's when the rebellious side of me came out. Drugs came in, parties came in. I just wanted to have a good time, and then all of a sudden I got a possession charge. Now the cops are looking for me because I didn't go to my court date. Now I'm looking at 30 days in jail, and I'm running from the cops."

Christian spent several years feeling completely lost, with no hope, searching for something. "And I just couldn't find it," he says. "I couldn't find it in success. I couldn't find it in money. I couldn't find it in girls and relationships. I couldn't even find it in failure. I couldn't find it in business. I couldn't find it in drugs. I couldn't find it in partying. Finally I found it in prison."

Arrested for drug trafficking, Christian was facing a 10 year sentence.

And on his first day, his girlfriend, Jennifer, called him and said,

"WE'VE JUST GOTTA TRUST IN GOD."

Christian chuckles as he remembers his response. "I was like 'God? I need a lawyer, babe.'"

Jennifer, who had also been into partying and drugs, had decided to quit after seeing a friend of hers overdose. She had only just started going to church with her grandma when Christian was arrested.

"He was just a little scared," Jennifer recalls. "He didn't know what to do, and I just told him he needed to get a Bible and we needed to just trust God in this. That's the only thing that was gonna get us through this."

Christian decided to take his girlfriend's advice. "I was searching for hope. I was searching for a savior. I needed to be saved. I was in a situation where I needed a lot of help. And the only place I was told to look for that ultimate help was in the Bible."

God knew that Christian would need support. That must be why, on his first day in jail, Christian met a guy who had already been in for five years, had a strong belief in Jesus Christ, and had a Bible with lots of highlighting and underlining in it. He offered it to Christian.

That was the beginning of a radical turning point for him. "I realized this was more than just a book," he says. "This was something that was real. This wasn't something to fool around with, something that you put off till later. This was something I needed to know now! I put all my efforts and all my energy into finding out who God was."

And he discovered that finding out who you are in Christ is the only way to find out who you really are.

Could it be that God had a purpose in allowing Christian to go to jail? If he had never been arrested, would he have ever discovered the truth of God's Word and the gift of salvation? "I truly believe it would have been difficult," Christian admits. "I know that God is able to turn anyone's life around at any time, whether it's from hearing a testimony or going through a circumstance. But for me that's what it took—four walls in a jail cell."

Meeting other people in jail was amazing for Christian. Several guys said things like, "You're that skateboarder!" or "Hey, I saw you on the news," or "You were like my idol when I was a kid." Christian just shook his head. This is not happening to me, he thought. What am I doing here?

After he asked Jesus to come into his life, however, his attitude changed. He began thinking, I can't wait to get out so that I can do more for the community, change people's lives,

HELP PEOPLE STAY OFF DRUGS, HELP SHARE JESUS CHRIST.

Christian Hosoi 9

CHRISTIAN'S STATS

Birthday:
October 5, 1967

Height:
5'6"

Weight:
165 lbs.

Wife:
Jennifer

Son:
Rhythm

Hometown:
Huntington Beach, California

Favorite food:
Sushi

Favorite music:
Worship music

Favorite Bible verses:
Romans 8:28

Favorite trick:
best known for developing the "Christ Air" trick, also likes rocket air

Career high:
turning pro at 14, owning his own company at 17

Sponsors:
Quicksilver
Vans Skate Shoes
Blacklabel Skateboard Decks
Spitfire/Rocket Wheels
Independent Trucks
Ogio Bags
Nixon Watches
Khiro Bushings
Ninja Bearings
Pro Tech Helmets
Active Mail Order
Jesus Christ!

10 Livin'It Testimonies

Christian Hosoi 11

DROP IN
or not?

JENNIFER STOOD BY CHRISTIAN the entire time he was in prison. She describes their relationship kind of like a courtship. "When you're dating someone, it's really hard to actually get to know each other, because it's just like a physical thing. "But for Christian and me it was all emotions and faith, since we didn't have that physical part. So we grew spiritually and mentally together, and I think that was so strong—stronger than like being physically there. I mean it was hard, but on the other hand we were growing so much that it was just awesome."

With Christian in prison in San Bernardino, California, and Jennifer in Hawaii, they spent a lot of time talking on the phone. Christian says, "If it wouldn't have been for her telling me we just need to trust in God on that first phone call, I probably would have been a real wreck, because I told her, 'I don't know if I'm gonna make it.' I was at that point where I didn't even want to live anymore." Their daily conversations helped Christian keep going on.

One day, one of those phone calls changed both of their lives for good. "I was on the phone with Christian, and my uncle said he wanted to talk to him," Jennifer recalls. Her uncle, Chris, is a pastor who had been witnessing to them for a long time.

Christian, Jennifer, and Uncle Chris had a three-way call on Valentine's Day 2000. Christian says, "At that point I'd been reading my Bible every day, and I know Jennifer had been struggling with the fact that I might get 10 years. With those pressures on us—with that amount of weight on our shoulders—we were ready to receive what God had for us."

That day, Chris led them in a prayer to accept Jesus Christ as their Savior. "All of a sudden, all that weight, all the pressures I'd been going through for such a long amount of time just vanished," Christian remembers. "It was like all of a sudden I had a whole purpose and a plan built-in inside of me. I knew it was gonna be okay."

Everything was different from that point on. Christian says, "When I would speak to Jennifer on the phone after that, it was like we felt so different. We acted different." Jennifer had a new confidence as well. She started praying and believing that Christian wouldn't have to serve the whole 10 years. They believed that God is a God of miracles.

180°

Just before his sentencing, Christian and Jennifer decided to get married. Again, Jennifer felt that God was telling her it would be okay. She went to her Uncle Chris for advice, and he encouraged her to turn to the Bible.

It was June 18. Jennifer was 22 years old. Somehow those numbers directed her to Proverbs 18:22, where she read, "He who finds a wife finds what is good and receives favor from the Lord." She knew she was supposed to marry Christian.

Although Christian was told he would get 120 months (10 years), it was really up to the judge. At that time, many judges were breaking the mandatory minimums anyway. Not only that, but the same judge who sentenced Christian was actually the one who had married them!

Call it what you want, the judge ended up deciding to give Christian only 70 months. "That was a super blessing," Christian says. He had already served almost two years, so that meant he had less than four years left. It changed Christian's attitude from "What am I doing here?" to "Wait, I can be used here!" He started witnessing to other guys in the prison, and they began to hold Bible studies every night.

PART OF THE FAMILY

One of the most incredible things about becoming a Christian is that you become a part of the worldwide family of God. You have brothers and sisters in Christ who care about you even if they don't know you personally.

After giving his life to God shortly after his imprisonment, Christian began doing magazine interviews and telling everyone how his life had been changed. Letters came in from all over the world from Christians writing and telling him of the influence his story had on them.

Jennifer helped Christian put together all the letters and stories showing how he was a changed man. All together, it helped them add up over 200 character reference letters they could present to the sentencing judge, as well as a recommendation from a sheriff who said that he believed Christian wouldn't go back to doing drugs after his release but would become a great asset to the community.

Bottom line, it was the testimony of Christians from all over the country that helped Christian Hosoi get a reduced sentence!

Christian Hosoi 13

HOSOI

A NEW LIFE
WITH NEW PASSION

RELEASED FROM PRISON NOW, CHRISTIAN HAS A NEW PASSION FOR LIFE—AND FOR JESUS CHRIST. HE QUICKLY GOT INVOLVED WITH MINISTRIES LIKE SKATE NIGHT, PROVIDING A SAFE HAVEN FOR KIDS IN DRUG-INFESTED, GANG-INFESTED NEIGHBORHOODS. AND THAT'S JUST A START.

"SKATEBOARDING HAS BEEN MY PASSION ALL MY LIFE—AND IT STILL IS—BUT MY NEW HUNGER AND NEW DESIRE IS TO BUILD THE KINGDOM OF GOD HERE ON EARTH AND TO LEAD AS MANY PEOPLE AS I CAN TO THE SAVING GRACE OF JESUS CHRIST. I WANT TO PRESENT THE GOSPEL IN A RELEVANT WAY SO THAT KIDS WILL OPEN THEIR HEARTS AND LET JESUS CHRIST INTO THEIR LIVES."

"WHEN I WAS AN AMATEUR SKATER WANTING TO BE LIKE THE PROS, IT WAS LIKE I IDEALIZED THEM. IT'S KINDA LIKE HOW I IDEALIZE JESUS CHRIST TODAY."

CHRISTIAN IS NOW USING SKATEBOARDING TO REACH OUT TO PEOPLE AND IMPACT THEM FOR CHRIST. "I DEFINITELY THINK GOD HAS A HUGE PLAN RIGHT NOW," HE SAYS. "I BELIEVE THIS IS A CHOSEN GENERATION, THAT THERE'S GONNA BE MANY SOULS WON. WE'RE USING EVERY GIFT AND EVERY TALENT THAT GOD HAS GIVEN US TO BRING GOD THE GLORY, AND THAT'S WHAT PEOPLE ARE SEEING—SOLD-OUT PEOPLE FOR CHRIST."

CHRISTIAN REMEMBERS VIVIDLY HIS LIFE BEFORE CHRIST—WANTING TO BE THE BEST SKATER, TO BE A PROFESSIONAL, TO MAKE MONEY, TO BE FAMOUS. BUT HE SAYS, "WITHOUT HOPE AND WITHOUT PEACE, WITHOUT A PURPOSE, YOU KNOW WHAT? YOU'RE GONNA MAKE BAD CHOICES. YOU'RE LIABLE TO WIND UP EITHER IN PRISON LIKE I DID OR IN HELL."

HIS MESSAGE TO OTHERS WHO ARE SEARCHING FOR SOMETHING LIKE HE WAS IS SIMPLY THIS: "TODAY'S THE DAY OF SALVATION. IF YOU DON'T HAVE JESUS CHRIST IN YOUR HEART TODAY, YOU'RE NOT PROMISED TOMORROW. AND IF YOU'RE GONNA WAIT TILL TOMORROW, TOMORROW MAY BE TOO LATE."

CHAPTER 2
TIM BYRNE

FROM RURAL MISSOURI TO THE BUSTLING METROPOLIS OF PORTLAND, OREGON, TIM BYRNE HAS FOLLOWED A TUGGING ON HIS HEART. SKATEBOARDING — THE PASSION THAT ONCE CONSUMED HIS LIFE — HAS BECOME HIS INSTRUMENT TO SHARE A MESSAGE OF HOPE WITH PEOPLE ALL OVER THE COUNTRY. GET A PEEK INTO THE BUSY LIFE OF ONE OF THE TOP FREESTYLE FLATLAND SKATERS IN THE WORLD.

NEVER GOIN

BEEP. BEEP. Tim Byrne rolls over to hit the alarm clock. It's early, but he fights off the urge to lie around in bed and instead reaches for his Bible. After spending some time reading and praying, Tim sets out for a two-mile run, then returns home to spend an hour on his skateboard. On many days Tim even follows this physically demanding routine up by packing his bags to get on a plane and travel to his next event.

It takes a lot of energy to keep up with Tim. "I'm 25, and I know I can skate until I'm 40," he says. "But I have to continue to practice and work hard with the gifts God has given me."

There's more than skating on Tim's mind, however—something that's sure to keep him going long after his touring days are over. "I know I'm called to preach the Word of

Livin'It Testimonies

God for the rest of my life. I'm never going to retire from that. I'm just going to do it until I stop breathing. I'm going to tell people about Jesus."

Tim hasn't always felt that way. Growing up in rural Missouri, Tim discovered his love for skateboarding at a young age. "When I stood on a skateboard, something just clicked inside of me. It was my way of self-expression, something I loved to do. Skateboarding was appealing to me because I didn't need coaches and I didn't need a team to go do it. It was something I could just do by myself."

His parents kind of liked the idea, too, letting him build a practice area at home. They saw other kids out doing drugs or getting into trouble, and figured it was better to know that Tim would rather be hanging out around the house or in a parking lot, flipping his board, just because he enjoyed it so much.

close encounter

Soon after Tim started getting into skateboarding, his mom was diagnosed with cancer. It hit him pretty hard. He remembers a pastor coming over to their house to pray for his mom, who was scheduled for surgery the next day.

But the next morning, as the doctor began surgery to remove the cancer, something happened that completely amazed him. The tissue that had been shown to have cancer in earlier medical tests and scans was already clean and healthy. When he cut in, he couldn't find anything. The cancer was completely gone!

After that miracle, Tim's mom dedicated her life to Jesus Christ.

But Tim still wasn't convinced. Skateboarding was pretty much the most important thing in his life. "Skateboarding was more of a teacher to me. When I connected to it, it was like I found my 'god' at the time. It was really just a part of me. It was my art. It was my expression. It was like, I didn't need God in my life. Skateboarding was good enough, and I felt like I was a good person."

After high school, Tim got a job working for the highway department, shoveling asphalt and holding a stop sign. He recalls, "I worked with people who were doing community service, people who had done various crimes, from robbing stores to killing somebody in a drunk-driving accident. I remember just thinking, man, this is what my life is going to amount to. There was something just still so empty inside of me."

ollie the void

Late one night, as he was flipping through channels, Tim stopped to watch a TV evangelist. He had always made fun of these guys, but for some reason this pastor's message hit home for Tim. He decided to give Jesus a try. He bowed his head and prayed the prayer as the pastor suggested.

But when he looked up again, nothing was different.

"I was bummed," Tim says. "I'm like, 'Oh, man, God. Where are you at? This isn't true.' I figured I was right. The whole thing's a fluke." But he decided to give it one more try.

He prayed again.

"God, if You're real and You're out there, I want to know You, and I want to know the real You."

The next couple of months, though, were ones of deep depression for Tim. Just when he had finally hit rock bottom—even to the point of thinking about ending his life—he found himself at a Wednesday night church service. He had been to the church with his mom a couple of times before, but that was mostly just to see the girls. This time it was different.

That night, what the pastor said seemed to be directed right at Tim: "Man, God wants to take what you're going through right now. He loves you right where you're at. God loves you." He invited the people there to come down to the front of the church and pray with him to receive Jesus.

Tim got up out of his seat, and right then he said to God, "I'm a sinner and I need you." He says, "Right there these things broke in my heart, and all that depression and stuff sank away."

"I understood then that the two-month period of time God allowed me to go through was a time where I'd be broken down, broken down enough so that I could understand what Jesus did on the cross and why. It was a clear understanding. I knew that those things in my life were sin."

One thing impressed Tim most of all that night. As he was walking out of the church, the pastor stopped him and said, "Listen, man, the gifts God has given you—they're not going to be wasted." Turning to Christ wasn't necessarily going to mean tossing out his skateboard.

Yeah, for now it just meant going back to work. But even that was different now! When Tim returned to his job at the highway department, he actually found himself feeling content. He was ready to go witness to the guys he worked with and tell them about how Jesus had changed his life.

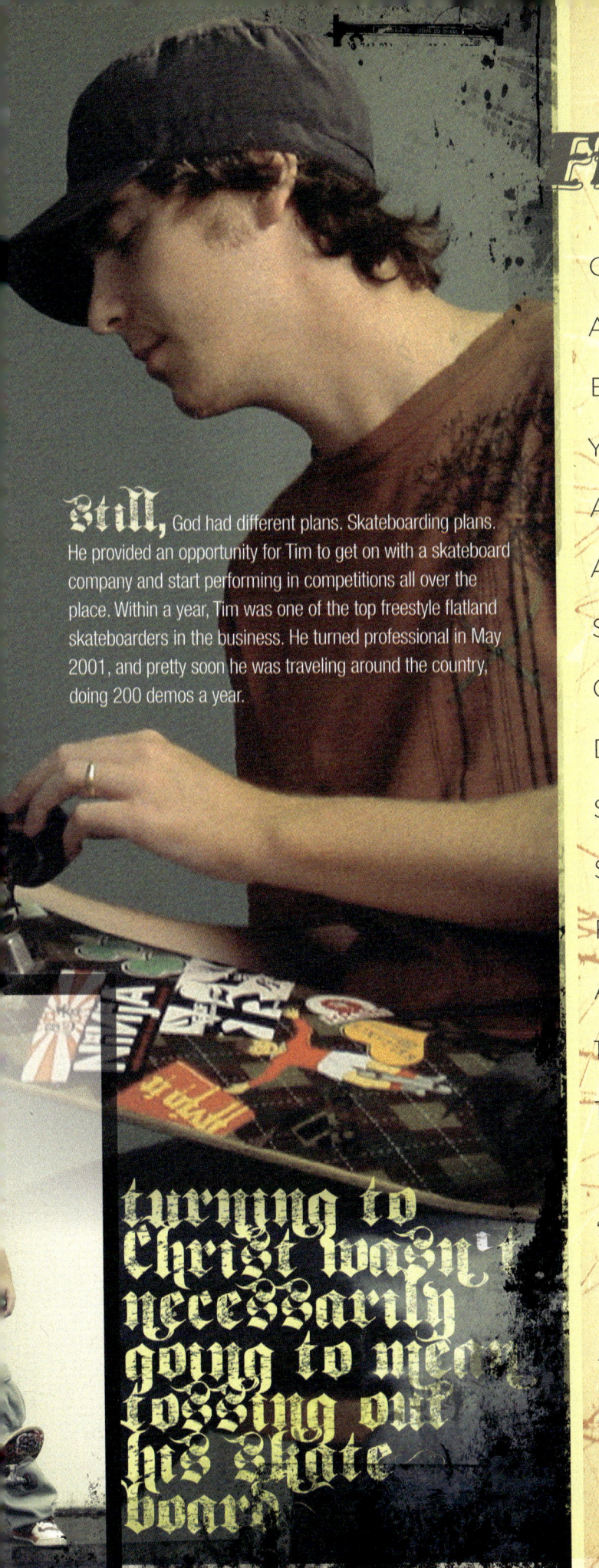

Still, God had different plans. Skateboarding plans. He provided an opportunity for Tim to get on with a skateboard company and start performing in competitions all over the place. Within a year, Tim was one of the top freestyle flatland skateboarders in the business. He turned professional in May 2001, and pretty soon he was traveling around the country, doing 200 demos a year.

turning to Christ wasn't necessarily going to mean tossing out his skateboard

FreeStylin'

ONE OF THE COOL THINGS ABOUT FREESTYLE SKATEBOARDING, TIM SAYS, IS THAT YOU CAN DO IT JUST ABOUT ANYWHERE. YOU DON'T NEED ANY RAMPS OR A COMPLICATED SET-UP TO DO HIS KIND OF STUFF. "I DO A LOT OF DEMONSTRATIONS WHERE I SKATE BY MYSELF ON STAGES. SOMETIMES I HAVE TO SKATE FOR A WHOLE 15-MINUTE PERIOD AND WRANGLE OUT LIKE 50 TRICKS OR SO. JUST GETTING THROUGH ALL THAT WILL GET ME STOKED." SOMETIMES CALLED 'BREAK DANCING ON A SKATEBOARD," FREESTYLING IS A GREAT WAY TO HAVE FUN ANYTIME, ANYWHERE.

Tim Byrne

TIM'S STATS

Birthday:
June 3, 1980

Height:
6'1"

Weight:
180 lbs.

Wife:
Liz

Parents:
Stoney & Shelly

Siblings:
Shane, Eric, and Veeah

Hometown:
Rolla, Missouri

Favorite Drink:
Coffee

Favorite Music:
Hip hop—"anything with a good beat"

Favorite Bible verses:
1 Corinthians 1:18,
Galatians 1:10, John 14:6

Favorite trick:
most famous for the triple rail flip

Career High:
being part of Livin It

Sponsors:
Reliance Skateboards
Tracker Trucks
Ninja Bearings
Reverse Freestyle Wheels
Jedidiah Clothing
King of Kings Skate Ministries
Skate Legion Shop

Tim Byrne 21

Livin it 4 Life

When Tim found out that Hollywood actor Stephen Baldwin was going to produce a video about skateboarders and BMX bike riders who are living for Jesus Christ, he immediately looked for a way to get involved.

Being a part of the Livin It DVD gained Tim even more recognition and attracted the attention of additional sponsors.

According to Tim, of course, the best part about being involved in Livin It was still to come! One evening at a barbecue after a full day of shooting for the video, his eyes fell on a beautiful redhead with blue eyes. Right then he felt that God just put it on his heart that she was going to be the one. When he found out that Liz wasn't seeing anyone, he decided to ask her out.

She said yes!

I was just thinking God, how am I ever going to see this girl again

At the time, Tim was still living in Missouri. "I was just thinking, God, how am I ever going to see this girl again, because I really don't know how I'm going to get out to the West Coast. She was in Portland. I needed to figure out a way to get out there.

"So I called the Luis Palau ministry out in Portland, Oregon. I knew Kevin Palau. I said, 'Look, dude, I'm in love with this girl. If it's God's will, it'd be just a cool way if I could get a job out there.' He called me back a month later." Not only did Tim have the opportunity to develop a relationship with Liz, but he also got involved with Next Generation Alliance, a part of Luis Palau's ministry that helps young guys who want to be evangelists find opportunities to share the gospel.

Tim and Liz were married in June 2004, and he continues to use skateboarding to reach out to youth. He has about a dozen speaking engagements each month, where seeing people come to Christ is the most exciting thing he does. He's even been able to see his father and his whole family accept Jesus.

Tim Byrne 23

"'IF I WERE TO SAY SOMETHING TO THE KIDS, IT'S **DON'T GIVE UP,"** TIM SAYS.

"Figure out what you love to do, what your passion is, what lights you up inside, and that's usually from God. He wants to use you. He wants to take you to the next level . . . for his glory."

CHAPTER 3
ANTHONY CARNEY

When he first learned to skateboard as a young teenager, Anthony Carney couldn't have imagined that he would still be doing it nearly twenty years later. Anthony is still going strong—making a name in the skateboarding world and sharing his experience with his faith along the way.

Anthony Carney settles into his seat, bracing himself for the long flight across the Atlantic Ocean. He is on his way from California to Europe to participate in a series of skateboarding contests. It looks like it will be a pretty uneventful flight—maybe he can get some sleep.

Sixteen hours later, Anthony is still awake—clutching his seat as his plane attempts to land despite some bad weather. His eyes widen as the plane hits the runway with a thud, careening from side to side and very nearly skidding off the runway. He takes a deep breath, wondering if this may be not only his first, but also his last trip to Europe.

The pilot manages to regain control of the plane, and

ANTHONY BREATHES A SIGH OF RELIEF

as they taxi to the gate.

Exhausted from his long, uncomfortable flight and the hair-raising landing, Anthony decides to try for some rest on the train. The lull of the train rumbling down the tracks is just starting to put Anthony to sleep when he is jolted awake—only to find himself staring down the barrel of a security guard's rifle. Somebody is yelling something about a passport.

With his heart racing, Anthony scrambles to find his passport in his bag, trying not to focus on the guns pointed at him. He finally comes up with it, and shows it to the security guards, who start laughing—"Oh, stupid Americans."

Anthony doesn't remember much of what happened on the rest of the trip. "I think I qualified," he says. "I think I made it to the top 20. There was like 200 people that entered and I made it to the finals."

His success at the competition gave Anthony hope that the problems of his trip were behind him. Unfortunately, just as everything was starting to wrap up, he lost his bags, including all his travel documents, and ended up being stuck there an extra two weeks.

Enough to make a guy give up skateboarding? Not Anthony! He stuck with it, and the trip to Europe ended up being a springboard for turning professional.

Anthony knows that none of his career in skateboarding would have been possible without God. He has protected Anthony every step of the way. Skateboarding can be a pretty dangerous sport, but Anthony has certainly beaten the odds when it comes to injuries—he skateboarded for 17 years with only sprained ankles and minor cuts and bruises. "I finally broke two fingers last year—they weren't really bad—and then some time last year I cracked a rib finally," **ANTHONY SAYS.**

"GOD BLESSED ME SO MUCH."

26 Livin'It Testimonies

Anthony Carney

Anthony's Stats

Birthday:
March 8, 1972

Height:
5'7"

Weight:
140 lbs.

Mother:
Carmelita Rodriguez

Siblings:
Twin brother, Patrick,
older brother, John

Hometown:
Buena Park, California—
now lives in Orange.

Favorite food:
Good Mexican food
or Carl Jr.'s chicken stars.

Favorite music:
Modern Worship Music—
Sarah Kelly, Delirious, Chris Tomlin.

Favorite Bible verses:
Galatians 2:20,
Psalm 19:14

Favorite trick:
360 Kick Flip

Career high:
"Seeing my name on
a skateboard—
it's just like, wow!"

Sponsors:
Ethos Skateboards
Destructo Trucks
Ninja Bearings
Active Ride Shop
Boarders For Christ
Vans Shoes
Spitfire Wheels

dropping in

Not many guys can say they've been a professional skateboarder for more than 10 years. Anthony has been unstoppable since he first learned to skate when he was a teen.

"My brother Patrick started skating a year or two before me when we were like 13 or 14," Anthony recalls. "Since we were twins, we were pretty much inseparable. He skated, so I had to start skating.

"He taught me a lot of tricks and from there we really grew a lot closer and we skated everywhere for ten years after that. But then he got a girlfriend and a car so we hardly saw him after that, and I kept going from there."

Patrick moved on to other things, but Anthony stuck with skateboarding—and it ended up being what God used to draw Anthony to Himself.

It was going to take some convincing to get Anthony to church. The only time he had been to church was with his grandma, and the experience had turned him off to church. "When you skateboard, you're kind of like a rebel, always looked at like the troublemaker, and I always got frowned upon early when I started skating, so I really didn't want to go around people that were just going degrade me," he says.

But when he was about 21, Anthony's friends started pushing him to try church again. He would be skating with his friends at local parks and schools, and they kept telling him, "Hey, there's this church I go to. It has skate ramps and stuff and you should come down and hang out."

Finally, his friends got through to him. Anthony decided to give God a try—and he hasn't regretted it! The thing that impressed him the most? "I realized these guys were real" he says. "The church was really, really cool. People were just in jeans and T-shirts and were totally in love with God. There were gangsters there, skaters, bikers… it was just normal people in jeans and t-shirts loving God."

As Anthony started asking questions and learning more about God, he came to realize that his old life wasn't satisfying anymore. He explains, "This [becoming a Christian] was right when I became a professional skateboarder, so I was flying everywhere and finally making some money traveling the world, hanging out with all the people I looked up to. But there was nothing there. The industry was just kind of disgusting, just nothing for me."

What the world had to offer just wasn't enough. "I'm just so glad that God changed my heart and I just gave my life over to Him."

What better way to remember something than to make sure you see it every day?

Each time Anthony looks in the mirror, he remembers two verses that have impacted his life. Tattooed across one arm is Galatians 2:20, "I have been crucified with Christ, I no longer live but Christ lives in me. The life I live in the body, I live by faith in the Son of God, who loved me and gave Himself for me."

Anthony says, "That's something I read when I first became a Christian and it just stuck out to me. And it just was so powerful I got it tattooed on my arm so it kind of keeps me in check day to day."

On the other arm, Psalm 19:14 stands out boldly, "May the words of my mouth and the meditation of my heart be pleasing in Your sight, O Lord, my rock, my Redeemer."

"That's another one that I read every day and it kind of keeps my heart in check where it should be" Anthony says.

GOING
FO

NOW ANTHONY USES SKATEBOARDING TO

share with others what God has done for him. He helps his friend, Chris Lauri, run a company called Ethos Skateboards, which began in January 2005. "Part of the proceeds we're going to give to various charities and it's just going to be an awesome way to give back what skateboarding gave to us," Anthony says.

Through Ethos, Anthony and Chris not only have the chance to do demonstrations and keep up their skills on their boards, but they also use it as an opportunity to tell anyone who shows up about Jesus Christ and how He wants everyone to receive His free gift of salvation.

"I came to know him as just a loving Father and He's showed me so much more than my passion for skateboarding. There's a lot of pressures out there, especially being a skateboarder seeing all the videos, seeing all the people out there thinking it's cool to drink and do drugs and party and stuff, but it all just makes them miserable. There is nothing more enjoyable in life than to be right with God."

Anthony's advice? "You don't have to do what the world wants you to do, like all these pros out there thinking that the way to really be successful is drinking and drugs and partying and stuff. It's not like that. Be who you are, love God, be right with God, and search out the truth—the truth is in Jesus because Jesus is the way, the truth, and the life."

JESUS IS THE WAY THE TRUTH AND THE LIFE.

34 Livin'It Testimonies

CHAPTER 4
SIERRA FELLERS

At age 17, Sierra Fellers has accomplished what millions of guys only dream about: touring the world, winning America's top skateboarding amateur championship, and starring in a movie directed by a famous Hollywood actor. For the first time, Sierra explains why all of that almost didn't happen.

pressure. practice runs.

Sitting on the ramps. Waiting. Praying. It's almost time for the last run of the 2004 Tampa Am.

More waiting. The signal. Then seventy-five seconds of pure adrenaline, throwing down a kick-flip, back lip, shove-it down the step-up rail.

The crowd yells— then holds its breath. Some guy out of Whitefish, Montana, named Sierra Fellers lands a perfect score. He comes from behind to win the most prestigious amateur skateboarding competition in the United States.

To be honest, the Lord actually gave me a lot of the tricks to do in my runs

Sierra's Secret

"To be honest," he says, "the Lord actually gave me a lot of the tricks to do in my runs.

"I prayed before I dropped in, 'God, what do you want me to do? This is kind of a big deal. I know you haven't brought me here for no reason. So what are you going to do with me? I know it's going to be big, because you don't do little things.'

"So he actually gave me the tricks," Sierra continues," It was as if he said, 'Why don't you do this?' Or, 'Why don't you try this on your run?' sometimes only ten minutes before my turn."

Before his last run at the Tampa AM, the pressure was on big-time. After winning the qualifying round, Sierra skipped over the semifinals and went straight to the finals. "They gave us only three runs. I was pretty nervous because I really blew it on both of my first runs. And then the last run that I had, I was the last person of the last event of the whole contest."

Sierra relied on prayer, listened for God's guidance—and now testifies that God gets all the credit for his victory.

Big Brother's Footsteps

Sierra is quick to publicly thank his older brother, Jesse, for teaching him how to skate.

"As his little brother," Sierra says, "I pretty much wanted to do everything Jesse did. I played soccer, baseball, and hockey, following in his footsteps. I started skating when I was eight. My brother taught me all the basic tricks and got me into skateboarding."

Their relationship wasn't always positive, however. "Jesse didn't really like me when I was younger," Sierra says. "He would pick on me and treat me like crud.

"But he turned his life over to God when he moved to Colorado Springs. He sensed God speaking to him one day as he sat on a park bench. He was into a cult at the time. He called my parents and told them he had come back to the Lord. So my parents drove out to Colorado and got him out of the cult."

Jesse used skateboarding as one way to rebuild his relationship with Sierra. "He's now one of my best friends," Sierra says. "He is the best role model I could ever have for an older brother. I love him."

Jesse and his wife, Melissa, now head up GX International. It's a ministry based around skateboarding, rollerblading, BMX biking, break dancing, and choreographed dancing that tours all across the United States and around the world. Sierra even toured with them before joining the amateur circuit.

SIERRA'S STATS

Birthday:
December 30, 1986

Height:
5'8"

Weight:
140 lbs.

Parents:
Michael and Leslie Fellers

Siblings:
Brother Jesse, Sister Shira

Hometown:
Whitefish, Montana
(one of America's small town tourist favorites)

World travels:
Australia, Belgium, Canada, Denmark, England, Fiji, Finland, Germany, India, Japan, Mexico, New Zealand, Netherlands, Norway, Singapore, Sweden

Favorite Food:
Asian—Chinese, Japanese, Thai

Favorite Music:
"I jump around depending on the mood I'm in. I hate listening to it on the radio."

Favorite Scripture:
"I've been memorizing Romans 8 lately."

Favorite trick:
"Anything I can land."

Career High:
winning the 2004 Tampa AM—America's top amateur skateboarding competition

Sponsors:
Mystery Skateboards
Mystery Wheels
Venture Trucks
Circa Footwear
C1 Clothing

38 Livin'It Testimonies

NS 8

Sierra Fellers **39**

VERTICAL TRUST

What Sierra loves most about amateur skateboarding is the independence. / "When I'm on a skateboard, even when I'm just rolling, I have such a freedom. That is my worship to God—just like music or dancing." / God has actually been a big part of Sierra's life ever since he was little. He clearly recalls the day he committed his life to Jesus Christ. His mother was driving the car and talking to Sierra about the Lord. "She asked me if I wanted to ask Him into my heart. I said, 'Yeah, but I'm going to do it on my own.' / "Right there, I looked out the window and I said, 'Lord, will you come into my heart?' I asked Him to come into my life when I was seven years old and was baptized not long after."

FELLERS FRIENDS

Over the years, though, friends began to play a big role in Sierra's life. Some good. Mostly bad. "All the kids at the church I went to skated an hour before and after church and youth group, so I wanted to skate, too. That really got me into skateboarding. / When I first started, my friends would come over, and all I'd being doing was trying to build wood ghetto ramps in my front yard. My friends would get so mad and so bored, they'd just leave. I've been skating ever since." / At age 12, Sierra's family moved to Florida. "I was a pretty bad kid at that point," he remembers. "I had a horrible mouth." It wasn't long, in fact, before his independent streak had turned into full-blown rebellion. "I started drinking and smoking pot with my new friends. Some were the big drug dealers in town, so I would hang out with them every day. All the time I knew it was wrong, but there was still comfort in it. / Honestly, up to that point I was empty. No matter how good it makes you feel at first, drinking and drugs always leave you empty. Just like when people get drunk, they're almost guaranteed to have a hangover."

NO MATTER HOW GOOD IT MAKES YOU FEEL AT FIRST, DRINKING AND DRUGS ALWAYS LEAVE YOU EMPTY

LIFE-CHANGING *Prayer*

Finally, at age 15, Sierra came to the end of himself.

"I remember waking up every day just feeling the exact same way as the day before," Sierra says. "It was a monotonous hell. Then the Lord met me. I snapped back into reality and knew that I couldn't live like my old friends any longer.

"I told God, 'I can't do this anymore. Take me, take everything that I am. I give my life to you completely, Lord. Everything that I'm going through—just help me, God!' And He did!"

What changed?

"The Lord has filled every corner of my life with the Word and praying," Sierra says. "My rebellion—He helped me a lot with that. He brought back my respect and care for other people. Because when you're involved in the world and you're everything the world is, you think the 'real world' is only yourself. That's automatic. But the Lord has brought passion back into my life for other people and for the way He's made me.

"It was a good thing I had parents who were very firm in what they believed and in what they knew God had for my future," Sierra adds. "That's helped me a lot."

ACCORDING TO SIERRA
THE UPS AND DOWNS OF SKATEBOARDING

WHAT'S THE BEST THING ABOUT SKATEBOARDING?

"It's such an independent sport that I can do it when I start doing it. I can do it when I have the desire to do it. It's not like I have to meet every day for practice at certain times. Most of it is independence and just the freedom in skateboarding."

WHAT'S THE WORST THING ABOUT SKATEBOARDING?

"Skateboarding is extremely frustrating a lot of the time, especially when you have a deadline pretty soon and your whole body hurts and you try a trick. The photographer is trying to get photos for a magazine or video, and it just doesn't work. Quite a few times, I've tried to do a trick for at least an hour and a half, trying over and over and over and just not getting it."

THE FUTURE
SIERRA'S PLANS

TYPICALLY, WINNING THE TAMPA AM PROPELS GUYS ONTO THE PRO CIRCUIT.

SIERRA WOULD LOVE TO GO PRO, TOO, BUT HE'S NOT IN A RUSH. HE'S BEEN TOLD IT'S IMPORTANT TO BUILD MORE NAME RECOGNITION FIRST. STILL, HE DREAMS OF THE DAY WHEN "SIERRA FELLERS" BECOMES A SKATEBOARDING BRAND NAME.

BESIDES EXHIBITIONS AND COMPETITIONS, HE WANTS TO KEEP BUSY GETTING MEDIA COVERAGE AND FILMING. SO FAR, HIS MOST EXCITING PROJECT WAS FILMING WITH HOLLYWOOD ACTOR STEPHEN BALDWIN. "I HAD A LOT OF FUN ON THE LIVIN IT PROJECT," SIERRA SAYS. "THEY BROUGHT IN A HUGE 30-FOOT CRANE AND PUT A CAMERA ON THE END OF IT. IT WAS DIFFERENT THAN ANYTHING ELSE I'VE EVER DONE."

WHAT'S NEXT?

SIERRA WOULD LOVE TO TRAVEL MORE AROUND THE WORLD, ESPECIALLY TO SHARE JESUS CHRIST WITH OTHER YOUNG PEOPLE. "I'VE ALSO THOUGHT ABOUT STARTING A COMPANY," THE CHAMPION SKATER SAYS. "I'VE THOUGHT ABOUT GOING TO SCHOOL TO TAKE BUSINESS CLASSES."

AND, YES, "I'M LOOKING FORWARD TO BEING MARRIED, HAVING KIDS SOME DAY," SIERRA SAYS. "I'M NOT THINKING ABOUT IT RIGHT NOW. WHEN I DO, I START FREAKING OUT."

FOR NOW, SIERRA IS CONTENT TO HANG ON THE RAMPS. WAITING. PRAYING. AND LISTENING FOR GOD'S GUIDANCE ABOUT WHAT TO DO NEXT.

FELLERS

Livin'It Testimonies

CHAPTER 5
BRUCE CRISMAN

BRUCE CRISMAN CAN'T SIT STILL. WHEN HE'S NOT FLYING ON HIS BMX BIKE, HE'S GRINDING ON HIS SKATEBOARD, OR TOURING WITH HIS BAND, DECORO. MEET THE CRAZIEST, FUNNIEST, MOST EXTREME ATHLETE IN THE

cameramen aim to catch and broadcast the latest action overhead on twin 20-foot jumbotrons. The 2001 X Games and 2003 Latin X Games champion is racing down the far northeastern corridor of the Rose Garden, home to the NBA's Portland Trailblazers.

His bike hits the arena floor at top speed and zooms up a ramp. It doesn't just fly into the air. Instead, it seems to launch into an orbit where gravity's laws no longer apply.

Bruce Crisman climbs higher and higher, spinning as lights flash throughout the place. His Adidas shoes float 4½ feet above his head as he looks straight down.

As if on an intense amusement park ride without a safety belt, Bruce and his BMX bike continue spinning away from the earth. The band Hyper Static Union plays on center stage, guitars blaring, drums pounding.

Then, with the pinpoint focus of an Air Force jet heading toward the deck of an aircraft carrier, Bruce pulls his bike back under him, finishing a 360 with seconds to spare. He lands at full speed, only to hit a second ramp and launch back up into the air while 10,000 fans go wild.

Sixty seconds later, Bruce races back onto the arena floor, sans bike, standing on top of the first ramp with a microphone in hand. In the spotlights, the logo on his black T-shirt seems fluorescent in the half-lit, suddenly quieted arena.

"I have Jesus Christ as my personal savior," 25-year-old Bruce tells the youthful crowd. "I'm not a perfect person. But the Lord is my savior and He knows my heart. If you don't know Jesus Christ yet, I'm talking to you right now."

It's something Bruce holds in common with the other headliners performing that evening at Jammin' Against the Darkness with evangelist Steve Jamison—NBA players, band members, and action sports stars. "We have been gifted by God so we can tell you about Him," he says.

He then reads from Galatians 5, where the Bible talks about the battle between God and the devil. "Don't give in to darkness," Bruce urges his audience. "Instead, choose God's light."

POWER OF A FRIEND

In front of a crowd or one-on-one, you'll quickly discover that Bruce Crisman is a bold and unapologetic witness for Christ.

"My parents were awesome when I was growing up. They were such good examples to me, and they always had me involved with our church," Bruce says. "But, as you know, it doesn't matter if a kid's going to church. It's what's in his heart."

Though Bruce grew up attending church, he didn't become a Christian until a fellow skateboarder, Jud Heald, befriended him at camp. Up to that experience, Bruce admits, "If I would have had the power to keep God away from me, I would have."

Instead, God used Jud to radically change Bruce's heart and mind. "Through Jud's example, I humbled myself deep in my heart, and it was like the Spirit was talking to me." Bruce had known that God loved him. He knew Jesus Christ had come to die on the cross for his sins. But it wasn't real to Bruce until then, even though he didn't really tell anybody about it.

A year later, when Jud and Bruce met again at camp, Bruce asked him, "Hey, do you want to go to church together sometime?" Jud had a funny look on his face, remembering the old Bruce he knew before. "You're a Christian?" he asked.

"Yeah, I am," he said. "Thanks to you."

"...TO DARKNESS,"
...IS AUDIENCE
...SE GOD'S LIGHT."

...N'T MATTER IF
...NG TO CHURCH.
...EN HIS HEART."

BRUCE'S STATS

Birthday: June 1, 1979

Height: 5'8"

Weight: 155 lbs.

Wife: Liz

Hometown: Tigard—a fast-growing suburb of Portland, Oregon

Favorite food: Korean, sushi (especially raw tuna)

Favorite music: "Honestly, I like everything."

Favorite Bible verses: "I'm really into the Gospels: Matthew, Mark, Luke, and John. Isaiah is very interesting to me, too. I've been into reading what Jesus Christ had to say, as well as the prophecies in the Old Testament—going back and putting all that in perspective. I think if more people, even non-believers, really sat down and looked at how much is in the Bible, how interesting it really is, it would blow people away. It's an exciting book!"

Career high: winning the X Games and Latin X Games

Sponsors: Adidas® Fender® Guitars Hoffman® Bikes

FRIENDS SPEAK OUT

"The first thing I think of when I hear 'Bruce Crisman' is a guy who is on fire for serving Jesus Christ. I don't think anyone can hang out with Bruce for 10 minutes without hearing about his faith and what Jesus has done in his life. Bruce is also the craziest, funniest, rockin' bike rider that ever lived!"

— JAMIE WRIGHT

"I guess the only way I can describe what kind of friend Bruce is, is to say that I would do almost anything for him. I think the reason is that he knows his place in this world and doesn't think he deserves any more or less. It's great to talk to him (even about riding), because he'll tell you about a cool trick he does from a technical standpoint in a way that puts the focus on the trick, not on the person doing it. That's just how he relates. Instead of either bragging or (on the other extreme) dismissing the topic and being overly modest, he'll (most of the time) talk straight with you about it. This is a direct link to his response to what he feels God has called him to."

— AARON SHEPHERD

"We played with Bruce's band, Decoro, last year, and we all agree that he has to be one of the most genuinely nice and humble people we've ever met. Him and Liz made it really easy to feel comfortable around them. Aaron's daughter has a hat that she calls her 'Bruce Hat.' He's a great role model—even to a three-year-old! We have a lot of respect for him and Decoro and hope to play with them again in the near future."

— JEANNE MITCHELL FOR THE SUZIS

Career Highlights:

WINNING THE X GAMES AND AGAIN X GAMES

FAVORITE BIBLE VERSES:

MATTHEW, MARK, LUKE AND JOHN

Bruce Crisman **49**

Birth of a BMXer

Bruce remembers watching biking competitions on ESPN when he was 10. He bought a BMX bicycling magazine, read all about freestyle biking, and then ordered his first BMX bike and some instructional videos.

"God really did prepare me at a young age to get me ready for what I do now," Bruce says. "Ever since I was four or five, I couldn't wait to ride a bike. One day my mom let go [of the bike], and I did it! And I haven't stopped since. As a kid, that's all I did every day. I was hitting humps and bark dust piles—the biggest jumps we could find as a kid. That's what my passion was."

But at that young age, Bruce wasn't dreaming of becoming a professional or appearing on videos. He was just into riding BMX bikes the way his father and his Uncle Randy were into their bikes—their motorcycles.

By the time he got to high school, though, Bruce started competing in BMX contests, kept improving his skills, and picked up several small corporate sponsorships along the way. Those sponsorships allowed him to keep competing. He soon realized, "Wow, I can actually make a profession out of this!"

So he worked even harder. And kept getting better. Still, no one was more surprised than Bruce was when he won the X Games in 2001. "It was almost like going back to when I was a kid. It was God's preparation. It was as if He said, 'You have no idea this is coming, but here it is—take it.'"

Winning the X Games gave Bruce the opportunity to turn professional. "I do take it seriously, but I'm still quite aware that I'm just a kid riding a bike. I keep it fun, for sure," always trying new styles and tricks "to keep it interesting."

WHAT WORRIES BRUCE THE MOST

INJURIES

KNOWING THAT YOUNG PEOPLE ARE WATCHING WHAT HE IS DOING IN THE AIR

TIME

"You could get seriously hurt that high in the air if you land wrong," Bruce warns. "Keep it simple and enjoyable. Learn control. Do curbs and street stuff. In other words, don't do what you're seeing on TV—not until you've been riding for about 10 years."

No, it's not easy being a professional biker. It takes a lot of hard work, a lot of time, a lot of travel and responsibility.

But if he had it all to do over, Bruce wouldn't trade jobs. Sure, he's big into wrestling, skateboarding, and other sports, but nothing compares with biking. "I like the freedom—that's why it's called freestyle. I can go out and ride around, and no one's pushing me or training me. No one's telling me, 'Hit 20 push-ups' or whatever. The great thing about riding is that you can just hop on your bike and do whatever you want."

Of course, competition is a different story. "The moment before my run, I have something planned out, and I have to keep focused. But I can still stay relaxed enough to talk to the other guys when I'm not getting ready for a run." This ability to switch gears quickly from social to hyperfocused is something Bruce credits to the multisensory disciplines he developed while studying classical piano as a boy with his mom.

Yeah, the piano. You never know how that stuff might pay off. (Get back to practice, boy!)

Spend enough time with him, though, and pretty soon Bruce will be telling you what it's all about. "We have no idea where our lives are going and where they're going to turn. You have to accept that," he says. "What it all comes down to is how you're going to react, man, what kind of example you're going to hold in that particular situation. Like, I know that the Lord doesn't send me to twelve competitions a year to win every single one of them. I'm just on a journey. That's why they call it a Christian walk. I'm not perfect, but I try to remember that I'm being an example. And when I do screw up, I thank God for the love of Jesus Christ and ask for His forgiveness. Most of the time, I also try to speak to a brother in the Lord. God's wisdom is poured out in fellowship. If we didn't have each other, what a wreck we'd be in. If there's one thing I can tell people," he keeps on, "it's that no matter where you are or who you are or how big of a status you have, you can't run from God—no matter what. God is constantly pulling you toward Himself. Whether it's through the example of a person or through His creation, God is constantly showing you how true He is and how true He can be in your life. If you haven't received that truth, I ask you to give it a chance. Today, reading this, can be that one opportunity, that one time in your life for you to consider the Lord as your personal savior. I pray that you do that."

YOU CAN'T RUN FROM GOD NO MATTER WHAT

52 Livin'It Testimonies

CHAPTER 6
ELIJAH MOORE

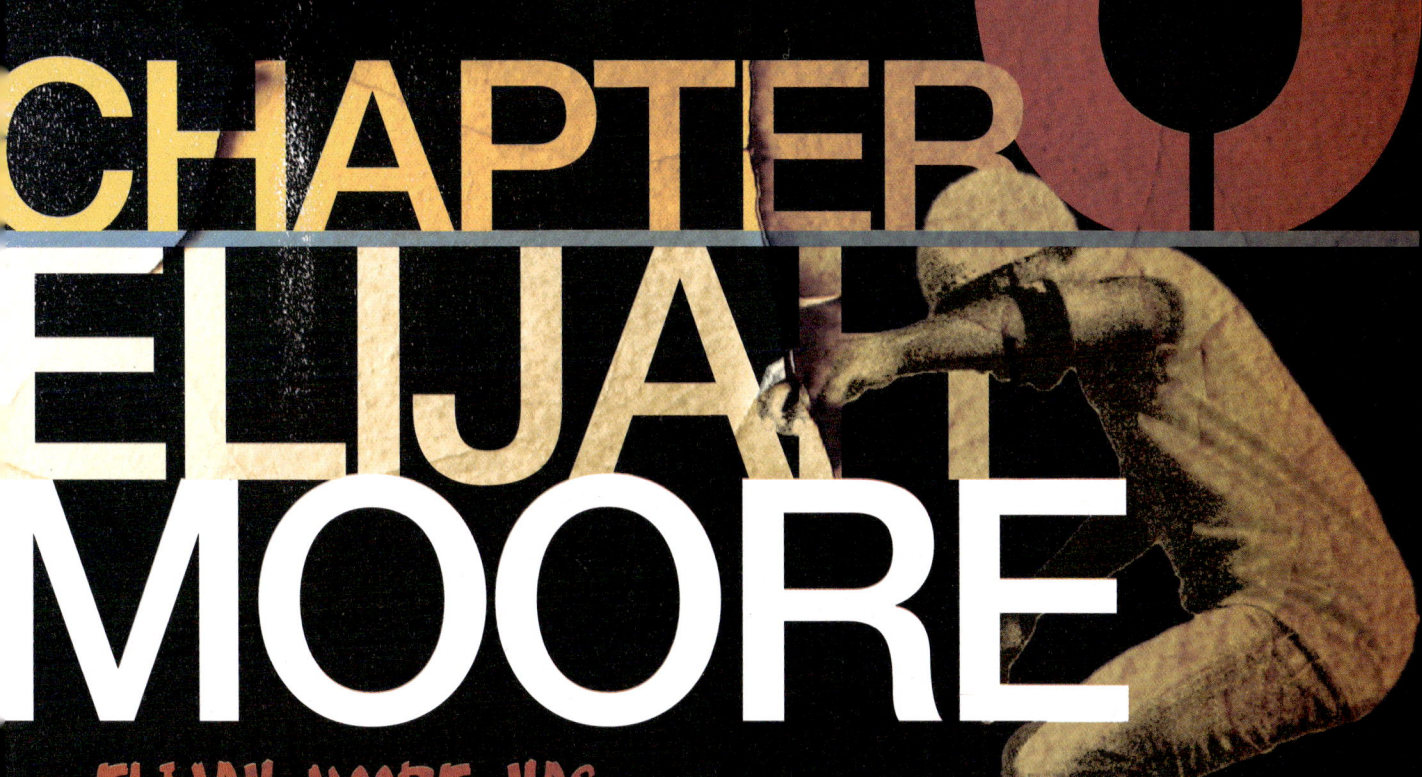

Elijah Moore has traveled down a hard road to become the athlete he is today. But it wasn't until he went down the wrong path and reached the end of himself that he found his dream job—and much more.

CAN I PRA

IT'S A HOT DAY IN QUINCY, CALIFORNIA. ELIJAH MOORE TAKES A DEEP BREATH AND WIPES THE SWEAT FORMING ACROSS HIS FOREHEAD. OKAY, HE SAYS TO HIMSELF. I'M GOING TO TRY THIS ONE MORE TIME.

Lining up his skateboard with the first kicker, Elijah once again attempts to clear the four-foot gap and the landing kicker to complete a successful kickflip to the flat (a.k.a. "fatty to the flatty"). The crowd waits in anticipation.

The takeoff looks good, but after flipping his board into the air, Elijah once again kicks the board away and bails. "I've done this before! What's going on?" his head screams.

Just then, a small boy, no more than eight years old, walks out onto the court. That's strange, Elijah thinks to himself. What is he doing?

54 Livin'It Testimonies

Y YOU?

"Can I pray for you?" the little boy asks timidly.

All the tension in Elijah's shoulders lets up as he kneels down and replies, "Sure."

With childlike innocence and sincerity, the boy lays his hands on Elijah and begins to pray. "God, will you help him land this trick? Amen."

Elijah smiles and thanks the boy, then without hesitation he goes for it one more time, nailing it flawlessly, and bringing out an excited roar from the crowd. "It was an awesome moment. God moved through that little kid."

Of course, he shouldn't have been surprised. Elijah has been seeing God work in some incredible ways for a while now—and it amazes him every time.

Elijah Moore

ELIJAH'S STATS

Birthday:
September 2, 1979

Height:
5'11"

Weight:
165 lbs.

Parents:
Elijah Moore and Pamela Henry

Siblings:
Tiffany and Charity

Hometown:
Garland, Texas

Favorite food:
Seafood—or anything healthy

Favorite music:
Positive music.
"I listen to all different kinds of music because I can be a moody person, so I go with whatever is good for my mood. Ultimately I like to listen to positive music because the Bible says that bad company corrupts good character, and when you're listening to music, you're like in the company of that person who made the music and they're going to rub off on you—if they're negative or not good it's going to rub off on you in a not good way."

Favorite Scriptures:
Proverbs 3:5–6

Favorite trick:
360 Kick Flip

Career high:
Winning the Vans Warp Tour for Dallas in 2001

Sponsors:
King of Kings Skate Ministry
Reliance Skateboards
Ninja Bearings
Fast Forward Skateshop
éS Footwear

56 Livin'It Testimonies

Elijah Moore 57

Big Dreams

Elijah's interest in skateboarding, just like his openness to God, was formed at an early age.

GOD OF WONDERS

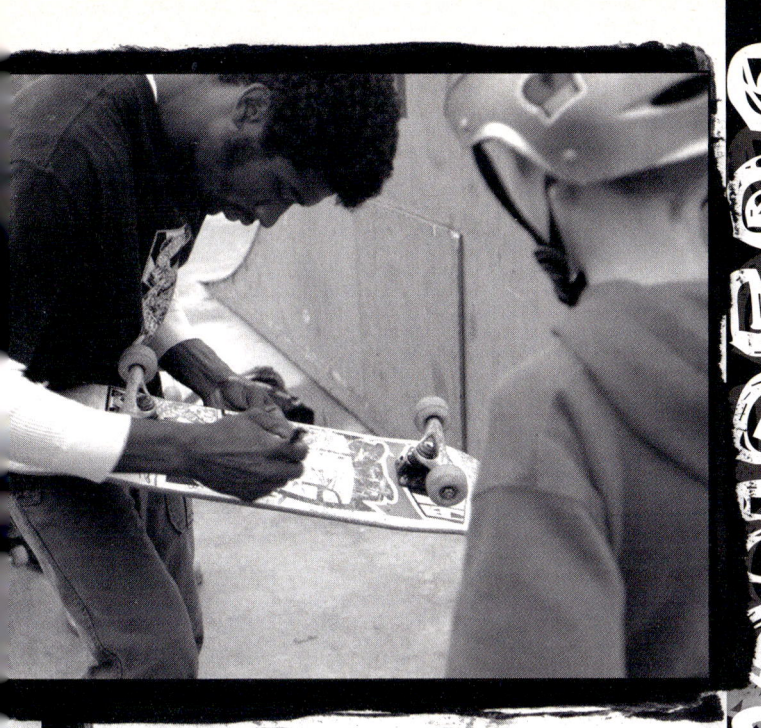

Elijah's interest in skateboarding, just like his openness to God, was formed at an early age. His family was poor, and his mother couldn't afford to buy him skateboarding gear. But there was a guy named Damion who lived in the apartments across the street, and he would come over and let Elijah ride his skateboard.

Since Damion was also African-American, the two guys were able to relate, and Elijah says he fell in love with skateboarding right then and there.

As soon as he was old enough to get a job, he started working and saving money to buy skateboarding gear. It quickly became his favorite hobby.

But after recommitting his life to God, Elijah started to understand who had given him the ability to skateboard, and he decided he wanted to use it to glorify and honor God in some way. So he started finding himself hanging out at skateparks, telling anyone who would listen about what God had done for him. He wanted other guys to see that he wasn't just passionate about skateboarding, but he was passionate about seeking after the God of the universe.

Witnessing at the local skatepark was great. Home and school and neighborhood are always good places to start when you're asking God to use you. But Elijah also had bigger dreams. He wanted to travel the world and tell people everywhere how God could change lives.

Elijah has seen God work in a lot of cool ways, both on the Livin It Tour and in his own every day life. Recently he needed to get his video camera fixed, but when he went into the repair shop, they told him it would cost five times more than he thought it would! For that, he could just buy a whole new one!

So Elijah headed down to the store, and found a nice new video camera for a reasonable price. But for some reason, he felt God telling him to wait. Even though he really wanted it, he listened to the prompting in his heart and decided to wait and see what God had in mind.

As usual, he wasn't disappointed. Just a week later, a former teammate called Elijah up and told him that he was looking to sell his video camera because he needed money to fix his car. He was willing to sell Elijah the camera—with an expensive lens included—for a great price, saving Elijah around $1,500.

"It was totally a blessing," Elijah says. "I didn't want to wait, but the Lord told me to wait, and when I did, I got way more than I ever imagined!"

Now with his favorite video camera and an awesome lens in hand, Elijah is ready to hit the road, and share how good things come to those who wait on the Lord.

While skating a demo in Dallas, Texas, Elijah had the chance to talk with some representatives from the skateboarding company Element. They told him they were interested in having him be one of their riders, and that they would get back to him within a few days.

But the days came and went, and Elijah didn't get the phone call.

Three weeks later, he was at a trade show in San Diego, California, where he met some of the riders from King of Kings Skateboard Ministry. They told him they were also interested in having him on board, and that they would give him a call soon.

Sure enough, they did. And Elijah accepted their offer. He knew they were a Christian company and that he would be able to skate and preach the gospel. But when Element finally did call back—soon after he'd signed on with King of Kings—Elijah began to regret his decision. "At first I was stoked to be with King of Kings," Elijah says. "But then after being with them for a number of months, I started to second-guess my decision and I regretted joining them, because I felt like I could have had more with Element—more recognition, get to see more of the world, stuff like that."

Still, Elijah chose to trust God, and before long he found peace with his decision. He began to see that God was giving him greater opportunities through the King of Kings ministry than he could have ever imagined. "I'm getting to see the world and preach the gospel."

"I get to ride with awesome riders who encourage me

TO BE A BETTER SKATEBOARDER AND TO BE A BETTER BELIEVER."

Hard to put a price tag on that.

Today Elijah is still touring with King of Kings, doing demos and talking about his faith in God. He says he likes to share with kids how God always has a special message for them through the Bible.

"Lately, God's been dealing with me on waiting," Elijah says. "One day I felt led to open up to the Psalms, and I noticed that there were several verses on waiting—waiting on the Lord.

"At the same time I was trying to figure out what the next step was for my girlfriend Tanessa and me, so I would pray, 'Lord show me what the next step is—should I leave this relationship, should I stick around, are we going to get married, are we not going to get married?' And I would wait for an answer, even though I started to get frustrated because I wanted to make a move one way or the other, either stick with her or leave and get on with my life."

It took Elijah a while to realize the connection between what he had been reading in the Bible and what God was doing in his life. He was feeling like his prayers about Tanessa weren't being answered, but in reality God just wanted him to learn to wait.

One of the verses that really impacted him was Psalm 27:14. "The first time I read that verse, I literally laughed," he recalls. "It says 'Wait for the Lord, be strong, take heart,' and then it says again, 'Wait on the Lord.' It's like he's saying, 'Did you forget already? Then let me tell you again—wait on the Lord.' That's what I needed to hear, because I need to be strong and take heart and I need to wait on the Lord."

Another verse about waiting is Psalm 46:10—"Be still, and know that I am God."

"When you're waiting, you're still, you're not just rambling around," Elijah says. "I realized that I need to be still—that when I'm still, I'm waiting. And when I do that, I'll see that he's working things out and I'll recognize his hand and his presence."

Now Elijah is sharing experiences like these with other Christians. "After I went through this whole experience of learning to wait on the Lord, I noticed other people who were not waiting. And they didn't have peace. They were trying to figure out the next step, and it didn't seem like anything was working out. I realized that this was something I needed to share with other people, because I'm not the only person dealing with this."

Like the verse says that he heard in a sermon one day,
"[GOD] ACTS ON BEHALF OF THOSE WHO WAIT FOR HIM"
(ISAIAH 64:4).

Livin'It Testimonies

Elijah Moore

IT'S A HARD LESSON
TO LEARN, BUT
HE'S FOUND THAT
GOD REALLY DOES WANT HIM TO WAIT

Elijah doesn't know exactly what the future holds, but he knows that as long as he trusts God everything will work out for his best.

That's a good Bible verse, too. (Romans 8:28)

CHAPTER 7
JARED LEE

YOU CAN'T SLOW THIS GUY DOWN. ON THE SKATEBOARD OR OFF, JARED LEE IS READY TO ROLL. IF HE'S NOT TOURING THE COUNTRY, DOING DEMOS AND TALKING TO KIDS THROUGH HIS SKATEBOARD MINISTRY, JARED IS REACHING HIS HOMETOWN IN NORTH CAROLINA WITH A SPECIAL MESSAGE.

it's tuesday night, and Jared Lee is hurrying through his homework, keeping one eye on the clock. He takes a couple of minutes to inhale his dinner, then grabs his skateboard and his Bible and he's out the door.

> *I know God is going to be with me and I don't have to worry.*

Ten minutes later Jared is in his friend Rob's garage—which really looks more like a skatepark, with ramps already set up and waiting for the guys to get there.

After an hour or so of practicing tricks and comparing boards, the guys circle around and Rob pulls out his Bible. As he opens up to the book of James, Rob asks, "So what have you guys been learning this week?"

Jared flips through James to refresh his memory. "Well," he says, "I really like the point about not just reading God's Word but how we should actually do what it says."

Twenty minutes later, Jared and his friends are deep into a discussion of James. The skateboards sit noiselessly beside them as the guys talk about what it means to really live the Christian life.

biggest blast of all

Most skateboarders get at least a little nervous before a competition, but Jared Lee knows he has an advantage. When he's getting ready to do a trick, he knows that the guys back at his skate Bible study are praying for him. He also knows he has a strength inside him greater than his own. He has the Spirit of God inside of him, giving him courage and endurance in the most difficult situations.

Jared gives credit to God's power for getting him through his skateboarding competitions. "I like the challenge of them because you have to deal with so much in those situations—mentally and physically," he says. But he knows he couldn't get far without God.

Sometimes Jared will begin praying about a contest months in advance. He says, "I know God is going to be with me, and I don't have to worry. It's a good feeling."

Jared Lee 65

JARED'S STATS

Birthday:
May 7, 1983

Height:
5'8"

Weight:
160 lbs.

Parents:
Jane and Wesley Lee

Hometown:
Waynesville, North Carolina

Favorite food:
Southern BBQ and sweet tea

Favorite music:
Old school rock n' roll and heavy metal.

Favorite Bible verses:
Hebrews 11:1
Hebrews 11:6

Favorite trick:
"I love just doing simple stuff."

Career high:
Winning Volcom Pro-AM mini ramp contest in Orlando, Florida, and placing 12th at the Tampa AM contest a couple of years ago.

Sponsors:
Untitled Skateboards
Adio Shoes
Independent Trucks
Dakine (flow)
Nixon
Playground Hardware
BP Skatepark
King of Kings Skate Ministries

"I LOVE JUST DOING SIMPLE STUFF."

Jared Lee **67**

blast of a bro

Around eighth grade, Jared started skateboarding with some friends who were into drugs and drinking. It didn't take him long to realize, though, that doing those things gave him a lot less energy to skateboard.

"When I first started skateboarding, I was so in love with it," Jared says. "I wanted to see how far I could take it." But the drugs and drinking were definitely getting in the way of his passion for skateboarding.

One thing really changed all of that. Jared was amazed when Rob Dolman—"definitely the best skateboarder in our town"—first started paying attention to him. He was older and got to travel all over the world doing skateboarding. But for some reason Rob started hanging out with him. He would drive Jared to different cities and skateparks where they could try out new tricks.

He didn't say much. He just hung out with Jared and showed him that he cared.

Growing up, Jared had been in a Christian home where his parents taught him to believe in God. "But God never seemed very real in my life," he recalls. Rob, however, wasn't just a Christian. He actually lived like one. "He just lived it day to day, and I could just see in his life the joy and the peace that he had. He wasn't hypocritical. He just lived the truth the best he could, and he had a big impact on my life."

He didn't say much. He just hung out with jared and showed him that he cared

68 Livin'It Testimonies

Jared remembers that he always sort of believed in God, but it wasn't a whole-hearted thing. It wasn't until one night after coming home from a trip with Rob that Jared got down on his knees and asked Jesus to come into his life. He prayed for God to forgive him, and asked, "God, if you're for real, you've got to prove yourself. You've got to make yourself real to me."

God answered Jared's prayer, not just by helping him get out of the things that were hurting his life, but—a week later—helping him find a Christian skateboard company that wanted to support him. God gave Jared a new outlook on life. He gave him his dream back.

And Jared's been growing as a Christian ever since.

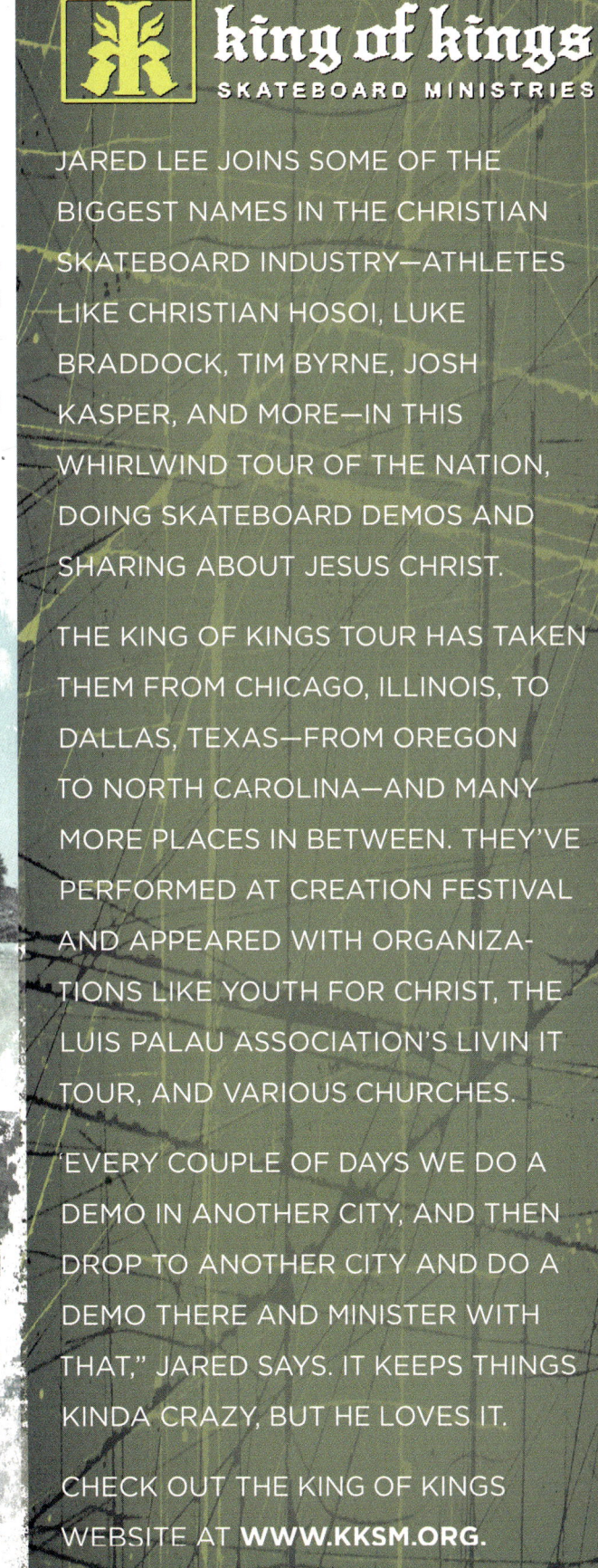

king of kings SKATEBOARD MINISTRIES

JARED LEE JOINS SOME OF THE BIGGEST NAMES IN THE CHRISTIAN SKATEBOARD INDUSTRY—ATHLETES LIKE CHRISTIAN HOSOI, LUKE BRADDOCK, TIM BYRNE, JOSH KASPER, AND MORE—IN THIS WHIRLWIND TOUR OF THE NATION, DOING SKATEBOARD DEMOS AND SHARING ABOUT JESUS CHRIST.

THE KING OF KINGS TOUR HAS TAKEN THEM FROM CHICAGO, ILLINOIS, TO DALLAS, TEXAS—FROM OREGON TO NORTH CAROLINA—AND MANY MORE PLACES IN BETWEEN. THEY'VE PERFORMED AT CREATION FESTIVAL AND APPEARED WITH ORGANIZATIONS LIKE YOUTH FOR CHRIST, THE LUIS PALAU ASSOCIATION'S LIVIN IT TOUR, AND VARIOUS CHURCHES.

"EVERY COUPLE OF DAYS WE DO A DEMO IN ANOTHER CITY, AND THEN DROP TO ANOTHER CITY AND DO A DEMO THERE AND MINISTER WITH THAT," JARED SAYS. IT KEEPS THINGS KINDA CRAZY, BUT HE LOVES IT.

CHECK OUT THE KING OF KINGS WEBSITE AT **WWW.KKSM.ORG**.

LIVIN IT

God has continued to bless Rob and Jared's skate Bible study. They moved from Rob's garage to a Youth for Christ skatepark, then had to close down after a year and a half because of fire code restrictions. But God has still provided. When one of Jared's former bosses wanted to open up a skatepark, he offered to let them use it. / Their Bible study's been going for almost five years now. "We get together and hang out and have fun and just look at what really matters in our lives. It's awesome to fellowship with skateboarders." / In fact, other skate parks have even come to them, wanting to know how to start up a ministry like theirs. God has given them tons of opportunities to use skateboarding to share about Jesus Christ.

TODAY, Jared's ministry has expanded far beyond his hometown. He's currently traveling all over the world, doing demos with King of Kings Skate Ministry and Untitled Skateboards. Both groups sponsor events where pro and amateur skateboarders come and do their tricks, then talk about how becoming a Christian has given them a new purpose in life. Jared's done everything from a giant festival in Beijing with evangelist Luis Palau to a recent Christian music festival in England. / "God is doing so much in the skateboard world right now, and my heart is for skateboarders," Jared says. "We use skating as a platform to share our faith and our lives, and then we openly give kids a decision to choose Christ or not." / Jared is well on his way to turning professional any day, but he plans to continue traveling doing contests as well as demonstrations—and sharing Christ with other kids who are into skateboarding but need Jesus even more.

Jared Lee **71**

ETERNITY

JARED'S THOUGHTS

LEE

"THE ONLY THING THAT'S GONNA MATTER IS YOUR ETERNITY—WHETHER YOU KNOW CHRIST OR NOT AND HOW YOU LIVE FOR HIM IN THIS LIFE, HOW YOU'VE SERVED HIM. I DON'T CARE WHAT YOU CAN DO ON YOUR SKATEBOARD OR YOUR BIKE OR WITH YOUR SOCCER OR FOOTBALL, IT'S NEVER GOING TO HOLD WATER, SO DON'T MAKE IT A GOD."

JARED HAS DISCOVERED THAT WHAT KIDS SEE ON SKATEBOARDING VIDEOS AND IN MAGAZINES ISN'T ALWAYS THE REAL THING. "SKATEBOARD TRICKS ARE ALWAYS GONNA COME AND GO. THEY'RE GONNA BE GOOD ONE DAY AND BE OLD THE NEXT DAY. PEOPLE FORGET ABOUT IT REAL QUICK.

"THINK ABOUT IT: PRO SKATEBOARDERS HAVE TO FILM ALL THESE VIDEOS, DOING THEIR BEST STUFF FOR ALL THESE DIFFERENT COMPANIES. IT'S COOL FOR LIKE A MONTH, AND THEN THE NEXT MONTH KIDS WANT TO SEE YOU DOING NEW STUFF, JUMPING DOWN NEW HANDRAILS. SKATEBOARDING IS ALWAYS GONNA COME AND GO LIKE THAT—JUST LIKE OUR LIFE IS AN INSTANT ON THIS EARTH. IT'S JUST A SPECK, NOTHING COMPARED TO THE ETERNITY THAT AWAITS US."

SO TAKE IT FROM SOMEONE WHO KNOWS AND LOVES THIS EXTREME SPORT: "PEOPLE ARE ALWAYS WANTING MORE FROM YOU, BUT GOD WANTS YOU JUST FOR WHO YOU ARE. THAT'S IT. HE JUST WANTS YOU. HE WANTS YOU TO BE HIS.

"I MEAN, THAT LASTS FOREVER, AND THAT'S SO COOL."

Livin'It Testimonies

CHAPTER 8
PHIL TROTTER

ALL HIS LIFE, PHIL TROTTER WAS SEARCHING FOR SOMETHING. HE TRIED TO FIND IT THROUGH SKATEBOARDING. HE TRIED TO FIND IT IN DRUGS AND GIRLS AND PARTYING, BUT NOTHING WORKED. UNTIL ONE DAY, PHIL FOUND WHAT HE WAS LOOKING FOR — AND A WHOLE LOT MORE.

Marty McFly grabs hold of the back of a green pick-up truck and lays down his skateboard on end, sending sparks flying. Biff and his gang are close behind, sandwiching Marty between the truck and their car.

Jumping off the board, Marty climbs backward onto their hood, walks over the guys from the front seat to the back, jumps off the trunk, and lands on his board again as it comes out from under their car. The bad guys end up in a pile of manure. Wow!

While watching the TV screen, Phil Trotter thinks to himself, That looks so rad. Someday I want to be able to skateboard like that!

And believe it or not, that's where it all started. Phil credits the daring stunts of Michael J. Fox's character in "Back to the Future" with first getting him interested in skateboarding. It made him want to get a board and give it a try. And he found out he was pretty good!

So skateboarding quickly became more than just a hobby for Phil. It became a lifestyle, along with all the other stuff that so often goes along with it—experimenting with drugs, going to parties, doing graffiti, and being rebellious toward authority. He found acceptance with the people who were into those things. They treated him like a real person.

But all the while, these habits were growing more and more destructive to his life. And yet, even in the midst of all these things, God was knocking on Phil's door.

"My whole life my mom told me about God," he says. He had heard about him in high school. He even went to church with some friends several times. But it wasn't until something else came into his life that he finally understood what it meant to be a Christian.

SKATECHURCH

During his senior year in high school, Phil was sitting on his porch, just hanging out like any other day, when something happened that set in motion a roller coaster adventure. "My friend asked me if I wanted to go to skatechurch," Phil recalls. "At the time I think I was high from smoking a lot of weed. So I was like, 'Okay, sure I'll go.'"

Pretty soon, though, he discovered that skatechurch was something radical. "Over a period of time I noticed something about the guys who worked there: they had a love for people. And it was kind of crazy to see that, because they had no idea who I was, but they loved me for just being there."

"Skatechurch" is just what the name implies—skateboarding and church. It's a place where guys hang out, do tricks on the ramps and rails, then gather around to hear the pastor give a short sermon or listen to some of the other skaters share about how finding Jesus Christ changed their life.

Phil went several times to skatechurch. He didn't get saved the first night, but he kept coming back. "At first I was kind of timid because I was like, 'Whoa, what's this about?' But as time went on and I started going there more and more, I just started to see that they loved me, and I kind of wanted to know why."

Phil had finally found what he had been searching for—unconditional love and acceptance.

THEY HAD A LOVE FOR PEOPLE, AND IT WAS KIND OF CRAZY TO SEE THAT, BECAUSE THEY HAD NO IDEA WHO IT WAS, BUT THEY LOVED ME FOR JUST BEING THERE

PHIL'S STATS

Birthday:
December 31, 1981

Height:
5'9"

Weight:
160 lbs.

Wife:
Ayako Asanuma

Parents:
Pamela and Edgar

Sister:
Samantha

Favorite food:
Japanese

Favorite music:
Instrumental

Favorite Bible verse:
Proverbs 27:17

Sponsors:
Adidas
Cal's Pharmacy
Venture
Scarecrow Skateboards

VERBS

Phil Trotter 77

Going Someplace

During the summer after graduation, Phil realized he had a passion for ministry. "I finally found the love I was missing, and I wanted to share that truth with little kids so they could grow up with the Lord in their lives and not have to go through all the stuff I went through."

And Phil decided that the best way to prepare for a ministry to kids was through Multnomah Bible College in Portland, Oregon. "My desire was to go to college, and God has blessed that. He's really used Multnomah, and he's used the people at Central Bible Church [host of Skatechurch]—he's used my mom, too—to really show me love and what it means to be a Christian."

Phil now volunteers at Skatechurch on Tuesday nights, helping out with the high schoolers. He's also involved with a skate camp through the Department of Skateboarding, building friendships with other skateboarders and looking for opportunities to tell them about God's love.

Phil plans to continue skating, and hopes to one day have a couple of kids, buy a house, and raise a God-fearing family with his wife, Ayako. He'll also keep sharing the gospel. "My passion is to serve God in a ministry—telling people about God and letting him work through me to impact their lives so that they can experience God's love, God's faithfulness, God's mercy, God's forgiveness, God's grace in their lives."

His message is simple: Christ will change your life if you let him.

SKATEBOARDING + CHURCH

SKATECHURCH

Think an indoor skatepark with a bowl, mini-ramps, quarter-pipes, and the works couldn't exist in the same building as a church? Think again! CENTRAL BIBLE CHURCH in Portland, Oregon, has opened its doors to the ministry of Skatechurch. Started in 1987 by Paul Anderson and Clint Bidleman, this huge indoor skatepark welcomes skateboarders from all over the city. Not only do they get to have a great time hanging out with their friends and working on their tricks, but they also get to learn more about what it means to be Livin It for Jesus Christ.

Skatechurch has 11,000 square feet of indoor skating area, including a bowl, a hipped mini-ramp, and two street courses with multiple ledges, launches, quarter-pipes, banks, euro-gaps, and hand-rails. Thousands of skaters in the Portland area have heard the gospel through Skatechurch, and over 1,000 people have accepted Jesus Christ.

CHECK OUT WWW.SKATECHURCH.NET FOR MORE INFO

Phil Trotter

"*It's been exciting.* It's been a long journey of trials and learning what's right and wrong, what being a man of integrity really is. It's a struggle sometimes, but ultimately God's love prevails and he does refine you and transform you into the person he created you to be. Once you become a believer, it's not like it all changes right away, but things do start to change. And if you let God into your heart, he'll give you a new heart and a new life. It's a process of learning to trust him with everything. I think if there's one thing that God wants people to hear, it's that he wants to have a relationship with them. He wants to love you for who you are and not for what you do. So if you think he doesn't exist and isn't real, then ask him to come into your life and make himself known to you. If he's not real, then nothing's going to happen. But if he is real and things do start to happen, just be prepared to open your heart to it. Because ultimately, that's the most important decision you'll ever make in your life."

ULTIMATELY GOD'S LOVE PREVAILS

CHAPTER 9
JOSH KASPER

Josh Kasper has seen it all, done it all, and had it all. Skateboarding in some tough competitions, dozens of demonstrations, and several popular videos for big-name skateboarding companies earned Josh a lot of money and recognition, but nothing really satisfied him until he found something worth living for—and dying for.

I just wanted at least one thing in my life that I could be good at, and that was it. So I kept on doing it.

THE CROWD WATCHES INTENTLY as Josh Kasper balances at the top of the stairs. The kids at the skate camp have been looking forward to this one all week. Josh takes a deep breath. He's done this demo before. Sure, it's a double set of stairs, but he can handle it.

Some of the other guys are standing behind him, waiting for their turn. Josh adjusts his helmet, then takes the stairs at full speed. Clearing the first set of nine stairs without a problem, Josh kicks his board away and begins to run down the wooden ramp lying against the second set.

But the steepness of the ramp is too much for Josh. Suddenly he flies forward head first. A loud gasp from the audience accompanies his crash, and the paramedics who are standing by rush to Josh's side.

Everything goes black. Josh wakes up in the hospital with internal bleeding, a lacerated spleen, and a broken wrist — but he's still alive.

"It was a really scary experience for me," Josh says as he recalls the accident. It was a trick he'd done dozens of times before, so the accident was completely unexpected. "It's sort of routine. When you've practiced for years, you don't really take a whole lot of time to prepare because you have so much background in that area. It just came as a shock and sort of freaked some of the kids out."

But Josh had been skateboarding for a long time, and he wasn't about to let an accident hold him back. A year later, he had made a full recovery, touring the country again, doing skateboarding demos and participating in competitions.

It's all he ever wanted to do.

early beginnings

While other kids were out playing cops and robbers or figuring out ways to insult their siblings without getting in trouble for it, Josh and his brother, Jason, spent their free time on a skateboard. For Josh, skateboarding became a way to escape from dealing with the pain of his parents' divorce. He felt like God had somehow forgotten about him and didn't really care what he did.

Josh and Jason spent many afternoons skating down a hill on their knees or just playing around with the skateboard. Jason sort of lost interest, though, when he went to live with their dad. But Josh kept doing it.

"It was something you could sort of do on your own and feel good about it. It's a real individual thing," Josh says. "I wouldn't always do it around people. I just wanted at least one thing in my life that I could be good at, and that was it. So I kept on doing it."

JOSH'S STATS

Birthday:
June 4, 1976

Height:
5'10"

Weight:
150 lbs.

Parents:
Ellen and Richard

Siblings:
Jenny and Jason

Hometown:
Santee, California

Favorite food:
Stouffer's lasagna

Favorite music:
Switchfoot
Hillsong United
Chrystina Lloree Fincher
Manafest (bec recordings)
Plus One
John Reuben
Toby Mac
and worship music

Favorite Scriptures:
Psalm 23
Philippians 4:4–9
John 11:25–26

Favorite trick:
360 flip

Injuries:
brain contusion, broken left radius, lacerated spleen; minor contusion of the brain; head slam at Carlsbad Gap; staples in the brain from attempting switch ollie 16 stair. "I only have a few of my nine lives left, due to my near misses throughout the years."

Sponsors:
Reliance Skateboards
King of Kings Skate Ministry
Tensor Trucks
Avalanche Ride Shop
Randoms Hardware

123
PIANS 4:4-9
1:25-26

Josh Kasper

Fame and Fortune

Lots of kids dream about making it big in skateboarding and earning lots of money.

For Josh, that dream became a reality. By the late '90s he was well-known for defining the cutting edge of the biggest and hardest tricks in skateboarding. And knowing he would need some sponsors to really succeed, he worked hard to gain the attention of several large companies.

One night during a huge skateboarding video premier, Josh was out skating some stairs behind a theater when a guy pulled up in a car and started watching. He was amazed at the stuff Josh was doing.

It was Jamie Thomas, a pro skateboarder Josh really admired who was known for skating big gaps. Before the show, Josh's friend Dorian Tucker had been telling Jamie about what a great skater Josh was, and Jamie had come to check it out himself.

Impressed enough to take it one step further, Jamie ended up introducing Josh to Angel, the owner of one of the biggest, coolest skateboard clothing companies in the country, TSA Clothing. Angel asked Josh to send a video of himself doing some tricks (called a "sponsor me" video).

That video eventually worked its way into the hands of Rodney Mullen, a part owner in World Industries. All the skateboard companies and sponsors were looking for who was doing the next big thing, and Rodney quickly saw that Josh did some incredible stuff. He offered Josh a spot skating for Blind Skateboards, possibly the biggest skateboarding company in the world at the time.

Landing a spot with Blind Skateboards gave Josh a huge start in the skateboarding world, but it didn't stop there. In 1997, Josh was featured in Trilogy, a skateboarding video that made him the envy of skateboarders everywhere. Fans of skateboarding loved actually being able to see skateboarders going down 20 flights of stairs, not just reading about it in a magazine.

At the time, Josh was still an amateur, but a few months after the release of the video, Rodney came to him and told him they had kids requesting a board from Josh Kasper. "I knew that meant I was going to get to turn pro," Josh says. "So I said yes!"

WHERE NO MAN HAS GONE BEFORE

One of the major high points in Josh's career was 360 flipping the Carlsbad Gap, one of the most famous places in skateboarding.

"Doing that trick sort of got me really well known in the skateboard industry," Josh recalls. "That's when my career took off and people started hearing about me."

Josh had to practice for a long time to get to that point. "You can't just pick up one day and want to go skate this spot," he says. "Carlsbad Gap is just known for how hard it is to skate because of how big it is." Few skaters have really done stuff there, but Josh was the first one to successfully complete a 360 flip on that site.

Josh Kasper **87**

That summer, Josh's career took off like never before. He toured the world, doing demos with the biggest names in skateboarding. He turned 21 in Sweden, was the first pro skateboarder ever to go to Iceland, and made other stops in places like New Zealand and South Africa. Before long he had skated on six of the seven continents. (Who wants to skate on Antarctica anyway?) / Josh was going places he had only dreamed about—and some places he had never even thought about! "There was lots of money coming in, and I was making lots of friends," he says. / Magazine advertisements and a part in another video (The Storm) helped push the popularity of Josh's line of skateboards off the charts. He now had nearly twenty different boards with his name and picture on them, and skateboarders from all over were buying them like crazy. On top of that, partly due to his success in The Storm, he even had his name on a new brand of shoe!

So where was God in all this? "He was kinda in the back of my mind," Josh recalls. "I was really angry at God from my parents' divorce, and I didn't really want to deal with him—which is funny, because he's the God that created everything. But I didn't want to take the time, and I didn't want to go to church or pursue my faith." / Josh's parents were both Christians, so he had heard about the Bible and Jesus Christ from a young age. He had prayed and accepted Jesus when he was eight years old. But after their divorce, as he found himself having to choose between his mom and his dad, Josh let his relationship with God get pushed aside. / He knew he was purposely ignoring God and just living for himself. "It was almost like I wanted to prove to God that I could take care of myself."

Yeah, Josh may have put God aside,
BUT GOD HADN'T FORGOTTEN ABOUT JOSH.

A few years after he turned pro, Josh started getting involved in partying and drinking because that seemed like it was just part of being famous. He was skating less and less, and it began to lose its appeal for him. It no longer satisfied him. / Josh's sponsors began calling up and saying, "You need to get back in there and do more demos and competitions and stuff or we're going to have to drop you." / Eventually Josh lost all his sponsors, because he just felt like he couldn't live up to their standards and expectations for him to keep doing bigger and better stuff. For years, he had been trying to keep up with what the companies expected from him, and he was getting tired of it.

Losing his dad in 2001 made Josh feel even more depressed. His life continued to spiral downward for a couple of years. / A lot of times you end up just hitting rock bottom before you realize that you can't go on without God. That's how it was for Josh. His dad's death and losing his sponsors had been huge blows, and no matter how he tried to fill the void in his life with other things, nothing worked.

Josh's mom had noticed how sad and depressed he was, and she finally convinced him to go to church with her. He did, and that was the beginning of a slow process of getting back to God. He got involved in a men's Bible study, prayer groups, and the young adults group, and ended up rededicating his life to God. / "I feel that God has a plan for each of our lives, and I just wanted God to show me what that was," Josh says. "I ended up getting baptized on Easter 2004 and just committed to have Jesus as my Lord and Savior."

It was soon afterwards that Josh met the skateboarders of King of Kings Skateboard Ministry. "It was crazy," he says. "I've never met anybody like some of these guys. They're all unique individuals and they all love God and just have Jesus as the focal point of their life. I didn't even know people like this existed. It's really changed my perception." / When Josh saw that he could use skateboarding to do outreaches and relate to kids, it had a profound affect on him. He discovered that other kids really looked up to him and other skaters. / "I realized that even though I screwed up and didn't do skateboarding the right way and made mistakes, God could still use my story to impact and change people's lives," he says.

Josh is now involved with King of Kings Skateboard Ministry, an organization of skateboarders that travels all over the country doing demos and sharing the gospel. / "There's a lot of possibilities with skateboarding being so involved with the youth culture," Josh says. "It's so exciting right now that when a lot of other things aren't working in youth groups and kids are losing interest and falling away— that's where skateboarding comes in. / The kids will come to just hang out and skate with us for 15 to 20 minutes and then they'll listen to what we have to say. They trust us. John 10 talks about us being familiar with the voice of the shepherd (Jesus), and we'll listen to that voice because we know it and trust it.

LIKEWISE, SKATERS WILL GENERALLY TRUST A SKATER,
OVER SOMEONE WHO IS UNKNOWN.

Josh Kasper 89

HASPER

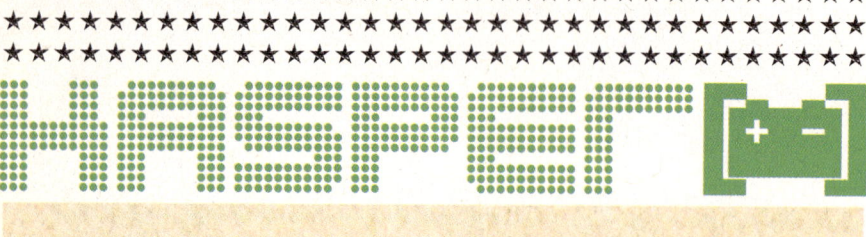

THE MAIN THING

Many skateboarders only dream of acquiring the fame and fortune that have made Josh one of the best-known skateboarders on the planet. But when you ask him about it, he'll tell you there's something else he has that's even better.

"God's bigger than all of that," he says. "I wouldn't trade God for anything I've ever had—not the money or the popularity or anything."

In the Bible, the apostle Paul talks about being an almost perfect person, someone who kept the law and was zealous for righteousness. But after he met Jesus, he said, "I consider everything to be a loss in view of the surpassing value of knowing Christ Jesus my Lord. Because of him I have suffered the loss of all things and consider them filth, so that I may gain Christ and be found in him" (Philippians 3:8).

"The main focus of my life is on Jesus Christ and what he did 2,000 years ago, and the belief that I have in him and in the Bible," Josh says. "Just like the apostle Paul says, all those things he had before are nothing compared to knowing Jesus.

"I can live my life confidently now and do anything God has for me, whether it's skating or telling my story. I know he's going to use me as a tool to bring people into the kingdom."

So Josh plans to stay involved in skateboarding ministry as long as he can. "My heart is to follow the Lord and just be a part of this ministry as long as my body is able to keep doing it. God can just use me to death, and I won't get sick of it."

Livin' It Testimonies

CHAPTER 10
JEREMIAH ANDERSON

AFTER STARTING HIS OWN BIKE SHOP WHEN HE WAS JUST 18, JEREMIAH ANDERSON HAD IT MADE. HE HAD PLANS TO GET RICH AND FAMOUS THROUGH HIS LOVE OF BMX. INSTEAD, HE FOUND OUT THAT SOMEONE ELSE HAD A DIFFERENT PURPOSE IN MIND – ONE THAT WOULD TAKE JEREMIAH FARTHER THAN HE EVER IMAGINED.

It's a typical Friday evening at the Anderson home as everyone gathers around the TV to watch the latest movie that Dad has brought home from the rental store. Tonight's film, however, is going to change forever the way 12-year-old Jeremiah looks at his bike and his world.

"What movie did you get, Dad?" Jeremiah asks with excited anticipation, having already seen the cover depicting a kid riding his bike. Curiosity is getting the best of him.

WHAT'S THE

"It's called RAD," his dad says as he slides the tape into the VCR. Little did they know that pushing the play button would set God's amazing plan for Jeremiah into motion. The movie is about a high school senior (Cru Jones) who uses his BMX bike to deliver newspapers. Throughout the whole movie, he does various tricks and ends up winning a big race at the end.

Jeremiah Anderson couldn't get enough of RAD from the day he first saw it. He watched it over and over again, trying to figure out how to do the tricks and then running out to the streets to give it a try.

"There was Cru Jones riding his bike—and getting rich and famous doing it!" Jeremiah remembers. "I said to myself, 'I have a bike, so I might as well give it a try.' That was 17 years ago, and now here I am today, 30 years old, and still riding a little kid's bike just like Cru."

Throughout junior high and high school, Jeremiah realized that he wasn't very good at any of the typical sports like baseball, basketball, and football, but he really enjoyed riding his bike. "I just didn't enjoy the team sports aspect," Jeremiah says. "I'm kind of an independent person, so I didn't really enjoy the thing with the coach yelling at me, telling me to do this or that."

Jeremiah's parents could see that Freestyle BMX was just the thing for him—an opportunity to use his creativity as a way to stay physically active. And as his passion for BMX grew, Jeremiah's parents became even more supportive, to the point of letting their backyard become the community skate park as Jeremiah's collection of ramps and obstacles grew.

92 Livin'It Testimonies

IT WASN'T UNTIL I HAD SPENT A FEW YEARS OUT OF SCHOOL TRYING TO BE SUCCESSFUL—AND FAILING—THAT I FINALLY REALIZED SOMETHING WAS MISSING

DEAL

Jeremiah's dad is child evangelist "Cowboy" Ray Anderson, so from the time Jeremiah was very young he was traveling around with his parents doing church programs for kids. His dad uses songs, puppets, illusions, and object lessons to present the gospel message.

One day, Jeremiah was listening to his dad's gospel presentation, and everything started to make a lot of sense. "He was talking about how God had sent Jesus down to earth to live and eventually die for our sins, how all we have to do is believe and accept the gift of salvation and we will go to heaven," Jeremiah remembers. "I thought, 'Count me in!'"

But in sixth grade, he started going to a public school where he got involved with some non-Christian guys, and ended up trying to think and act like them to fit in. He strayed away from God for a time.

"I went through a rebellious stage where knowing Jesus really wasn't important or cool. It wasn't until I had spent a few years out of school trying to be successful—and failing—that I finally realized something was missing. It was at that point I finally began to take all the things I had learned about God, salvation, and Jesus' sacrifice for my sins, and I began having a personal relationship with Christ."

As a senior in high school, Jeremiah had no idea what he wanted to do with his life. He graduated in the top ten percent of his class, and everyone expected him to go off to college. At his graduation reception, all his friends and family were asking, "Where are you going to go to school?" When Jeremiah told them, "I'm not going to go to college. I'm just going to ride my bike," everyone laughed.

But that's exactly what Jeremiah did.

He started a bike shop called Absurdly Insane Clothing and Bike, and decided he was going to make money and ride his bike forever.

In 1995 he started doing shows to promote his company, changing its name to Chaos on Wheels. "At that time my company was all about being a profitable business. I had plans to do stunt shows, build a skatepark, and expand the bike shop I was running." But after three or four years of pursuing his goal, Jeremiah found himself still unable to pay the bills. He got a job at Wal-Mart to try to make ends meet.

At 21 years old, Jeremiah was starting to feel like his life was pointless.

Jeremiah Anderson 93

JEREMIAH'S STATS

Birthday:
January 20, 1976

Height:
6'1"

Weight:
175 lbs.

Wife:
Jennifer

Parents:
Ray and Lois

Kids:
Ethan, Micah and Levi

Hometown:
Elmore, Minnesota

Lives in:
Joplin, Missouri

Favorite food:
Cajun food,
especially boiled crawfish

Favorite music:
hard-core metal
(favorites are Living Sacrifice
and Nodes of Ranvier)

Favorite Bible verses:
Philippians 4:13

Favorite Tricks:
x-up variations
360s
the Decade

CHAOS ON WHEELS

back in high school, Jeremiah sometimes spent his study hall time doodling and drawing stuff, writing stories about BMX guys. One day a couple years after he graduated, he was flipping through some of those notebooks when he came across a picture of a guy doing a trick, and below it was this caption: "chaos on wheels."

At the time, Jeremiah's bike shop was starting to do some shows, and since they had skateboarders and BMXers and inline skaters, he needed a new name that would encompass everybody. Since everyone had wheels, he decided that Chaos on Wheels was the perfect name.

"Originally our shows were really chaotic," Jeremiah says. "When we first started doing it, we had no idea what a show should look like. We were just a bunch of guys on bikes and skateboards and rollerblades just going back and forth on ramps and most of the time falling down."

Even after Chaos on Wheels developed into the ministry it is today, the name stuck. "Everybody seems to like it, so we kept it. We still get comments like 'I love that name. It's great.'"

Check out www.chaosonwheels.com for more information.

Favorite tricks:
X-UP
VARIATIONS
360S
THE
DECADE

FAVORITE BIBLE VERSES:
PHILIPPIANS
4:13

Jeremiah Anderson

MORE THAN YOU THINK

"I remember being ready to give up the whole bike thing because I just didn't feel it was going to work," Jeremiah recalls. "One night I sat down in my room and asked God why he was cheating me out of success and happiness. I felt I had worked hard and was a good person. I went to church. I had never smoked, drank, or done drugs, I had stayed away from the temptations of girls and sex. Yet I wasn't happy and felt like a failure."

It was then that God began to show him that he was doing everything for the wrong reasons. He realized that he needed to glorify God above anything else.

One incident in particular confirmed this to him.

For a long time, Jeremiah had been using pretty much anyone he could find for his shows who could ride a bike, skate, or in-line, without much thought about who they were as people. Some of the guys, though, used some rough language and would go under the ramps to smoke.

"I didn't really think it was a big deal," Jeremiah says. "Then one day I was talking with a family I knew, and they said their little boys went home after the show and started rolling up paper like cigarettes and started using some of the words they had heard there. The little boys said they wanted to be like the guys they saw at the show."

Before that moment Jeremiah hadn't realized the awesome opportunity God had given him with Chaos on Wheels. "I had been wasting God's gift to try to further my agenda of money and worldly success, when I could have been using the talents he gave me to change people's lives for eternity."

So Jeremiah started looking for ways to use Chaos on Wheels as a ministry, searching for riders who shared his desire to use their love for BMX to share Jesus with others. "It took a bad experience for me to realize all that God had planned for my life. He's been able to accomplish so much more than I ever could by chasing after my own selfish desires."

It wasn't easy, though. For seven years, Jeremiah continued to work full-time at Wal-Mart, doing shows whenever he could get the time off, waiting for the day when he could pursue Chaos on Wheels as a full-time ministry. God finally opened the doors for him in 2002.

HOW 2-B LIVIN IT

Today through Chaos on Wheels, Jeremiah has seen God do some pretty incredible things.

He's watched riders—who weren't even Christians when they started doing the demos—become some of the strongest Christians on the team from being around the other guys, from seeing it firsthand. Some people told him it was a bad idea to have non-Christian riders, but Jeremiah felt that God wanted him to befriend them, to help them see why the Christian BMXers did what they did.

He's also watched tons of kids come forward at the demos and leave changed forever. "These kids come in here, and you can see it in their eyes that they don't care. They're just here to see a show and nothing more. But before they leave, they see the gospel presentation and they come forward. Some of them almost have tears in their eyes. They finally see what's missing from their life."

Chaos on Wheels has grown a lot in ten years. Jeremiah's brother, Matthew, coordinates a second team of riders and helps Jeremiah out with speaking duties at the demonstrations. Also joining Jeremiah are his wife, Jennifer, and his three young sons, Ethan, Micah, and Levi. Jennifer handles the merchandise table, takes pictures of the shows, and manages the website.

Recently Chaos on Wheels has joined the Livin It Tour to provide riders and ramps for demonstrations in cities all over the United States. "I had an opportunity to ride my bike in front of hundreds of thousands of people this last year. It's just amazing," Jeremiah says.

Today, Chaos on Wheels is based at Autumn Ramp Park in Joplin, Missouri, where Jeremiah is manager. "Even though I'm not traveling as much, I get to recruit and disciple new riders and send them out on the road. I guess Chaos on Wheels has really given me the opportunity to take all my successes and failures and use those experiences to help others."

GOD BEGAN TO SHOW ME THAT I WAS DOING EVERYTHING FOR THE WRONG REASONS

CHAOS ON WHEELS HAS HELPED ME TO REALIZE MY DREAM

Funny how seeing God at work can change things for you. "I thought if I got rich and famous and made a lot of money and rode my bike, I would be happy," Jeremiah tells the crowds at the demos. "Everything I tried to fill up my life with—through BMX or music or money or whatever—nothing worked. But I started using my bike riding as a ministry and kind of rededicated my life," he says. "When I did that, my life didn't automatically just change and become better. But slowly things started to make sense, and everything I did seemed to have purpose. Now here I am ten years later, living out my dreams. But it's not because of what I did. It's what God did through me. We all have failures and make mistakes but God can pick us up, brush us off, and change us. He can make us what He wants us to be. God has a purpose for all of us."

GOD HAS A PURPOSE FOR ALL OF US

98 Livin'It Testimonies

CHAPTER 11
CHRIS WEIGELE

CHRIS WEIGELE HAS THE COOLEST JOB IN THE WORLD. HE TRAVELS ALL OVER THE COUNTRY DOING HIS TWO FAVORITE THINGS — SKATEBOARDING AND SHARING WITH KIDS ABOUT HIS FAITH. AND HE CREDITS ONE PERSON WITH MAKING IT ALL POSSIBLE.

THE 2 TH

"GOD HAS AMAZING PLANS FOR YOU,"

CHRIS WEIGELE SAID AS HE PUT HIS HAND ON THE SHOULDER OF A 19-YEAR-OLD BOY AND LOOKED INTENTLY INTO HIS FACE.

HUNDREDS OF KIDS HAD COME OUT THAT DAY TO WATCH THE SKATEBOARDING DEMONSTRATION, AND ONE OF THEM IN PARTICULAR HAD CAUGHT CHRIS'S ATTENTION. THIS KID HAD BEEN IN A LOT OF TROUBLE—HAD EVEN SPENT A FEW NIGHTS IN JAIL—AND HE DIDN'T WANT TO GO BACK TO HIS OLD LIFESTYLE. HE CAME FORWARD AT THE END OF THE DEMO TO REDEDICATE HIS LIFE TO GOD.

SINCE CHRIS WAS ALSO 19, HE FELT A SPECIAL CONNECTION TO THIS HURTING KID. HE SHARED HIS FAVORITE VERSE, JEREMIAH 29:11, WHICH TALKS ABOUT HOW GOD HAS PLANS FOR EACH OF US—PLANS TO GIVE US HOPE AND A FUTURE. "BUT WE'RE NEVER GOING TO KNOW THOSE PLANS UNLESS WE STOP AND PAY ATTENTION TO GOD AND HAVE A FULL RELATIONSHIP WITH HIM," CHRIS SAYS.

CHRIS HAS SHARED THIS VERSE MANY TIMES AT EVENTS ALL OVER THE COUNTRY. HE TOURS WITH A SKATEBOARDING MINISTRY CALLED KING OF KINGS, WHICH USES SKATEBOARDING TO EXPOSE KIDS TO THE GOSPEL MESSAGE OF JESUS CHRIST.

Although he used to do BMX and other sports, Chris got involved with skateboarding because of his older brother, Robbie. Robbie was one of the first riders for King of Kings, and as he got into it, Chris followed along. "I would just do everything my older brother did," Chris remembers. "I didn't even really like it at first, but I just did it so I could be cool, so I could be like my older brother."

But it soon became more than that. As he continued to get better on his skateboard, Chris discovered that it was actually kind of fun. So even though Robbie eventually got married and then started getting into firefighting, making it hard for him to do much skating anymore, Chris has continued to be involved with skateboard ministry.

Touring with King of Kings is actually a full-time job, and although he doesn't get paid much (just enough to live on), Chris says it's worth it. "The two things I love the most in life, I get to do them. I get to skate and I get to share the love of Christ with kids all over the world."

CHRIS'S STATS

Birthday:
July 29, 1985

Height:
5'10"

Weight:
135 lbs.

Parents:
Rick and Miriam Weigele

Siblings:
Robbie
and Elizabeth

Hometown:
Chandler, Arizona

Favorite food:
seafood and
Mexican food

Favorite music:
all kinds—
especially the band Coldplay

Favorite Scriptures:
Jeremiah 29:11-13

Favorite trick:
fakie big spin heelflip and
switch flip back tail

Injuries:
fractured jaw
knocked-out front teeth

Sponsors:
King of Kings Skateboard Ministry
Reliance Skateboards
Salvation Skate
Jedediah Clothing

Livin' It Testimonies

ISAIAH 29:11-13

Chris Weigele 103

SUMMER OF SKATEBOARDING

Even though Chris grew up in a Christian family, going to church every Sunday and accepting Christ into his life when he was young, it didn't really sink in until he was a teenager. / "I knew that I was going to go to heaven," Chris says, "but I didn't know that along with it came a relationship with God." When he was 13, though, he attended a Christian camp where he realized that he needed to stop living for himself. / Then the summer after he graduated from high school, Chris had the opportunity of a lifetime. His brother had gone to Bible college with a guy named Graham who was involved with skate ministry in England. He connected with Chris, and Chris ended up spending the summer in England doing ministry with him. / "Graham was a mentor to me. He showed me what it meant to be a godly man and to live for Christ, not just to call yourself a Christian and go about your business and do whatever you want to try to fulfill your own wants and needs."

CHRIS and Graham did all kinds of events that summer in England. Graham would contact a church and they would set something up. Some of the churches already had ramps, so he and Chris just had to show up. But before every event they would put up fliers, go around town, and just talk to kids. They went from city to city, doing demonstrations and showing the Livin It DVD. / In August, there was a Creation Festival in Devon, England, put on by Calvary Chapel, featuring tons of great speakers and bands. Graham and Chris got to build a skatepark there and do demos all week attracting hundreds of kids. / God was really working in Chris's life that summer. "I kind of feel like he took me out there to change me and to change my heart and to prepare me for this ministry I'm in right now," he says. It was in England that Chris first came across Jeremiah 29:11 and decided to make it his favorite verse. It says, "'For I know the plans I have for you,' declares the Lord, 'plans to prosper you and not to harm you, plans to give you hope and a future.'" / Chris explains, "When I saw that, I was so stoked because God has plans for all of our lives. For Chris, that meant being involved in skate ministry . . . for good. / "When I got out of high school, I didn't have very good grades and I wasn't planning on going to college right away. It was like God had way bigger plans for me than going to college or just having, like, a 9-to-5 job. He just showed me that wasn't for me, and he gave me this skateboarding ministry which is just awesome."

Chris Weigele **105**

message fr

Now Chris is back in the United States, still working with King of Kings. They've performed at some huge events, like a recent evangelistic festival in Texas that attracted 200,000 people.

"We had so many people coming forward," Chris recalls. "Anywhere from, like, grandparents to little children—it was awesome to see that age range. I actually got to talk to this older couple. It was cool to be able to share God's love with them and just to see the Spirit moving in them when they came forward with tears in their eyes, just knowing that something was touching their hearts."

Besides being a sideshow at larger events, King of Kings also does smaller demos that bring 2,000 to 3,000 people out, just to see Chris and the other skateboarders do their amazing tricks.

It can definitely be a little nerve-racking to be skating in front of that many people, Chris admits. "I still get kinda nervous sometimes, but I've definitely gotten used to being able to speak and skate in front of people."

om sk8

have definitely gotten used to being able to speak and relate in front people

livin it

ATLANTA. CHICAGO. DALLAS. BUFFALO. OMAHA.

DURING THE SUMMER, CHRIS WEIGELE IS IN A DIFFERENT CITY NEARLY EVERY WEEKEND WITH THE *LIVIN IT* TOUR, DOING SKATEBOARDING DEMONSTRATIONS AND SHARING THE GOSPEL WITH KIDS.

CHRIS JOINS OTHER SKATEBOARDERS FROM KING OF KINGS, AS WELL AS BMXERS FROM CHAOS ON WHEELS, STOPPING IN OVER 20 CITIES EACH SUMMER. THE GROUPS COME TOGETHER TO DO SOME INCREDIBLE SHOWS IN FRONT OF THOUSANDS OF KIDS WHO ARE INTERESTED IN EXTREME SPORTS. AFTERWARDS, THE ATHLETES SHARE THEIR TESTIMONIES AND TALK ABOUT WHAT IT MEANS TO BE LIVIN' LIFE FOR JESUS CHRIST.

CHECK OUT **WWW.LIVINIT.COM** TO SEE IF THE LIVIN IT TOUR IS COMING TO A CITY NEAR YOU!

Chris Weigele

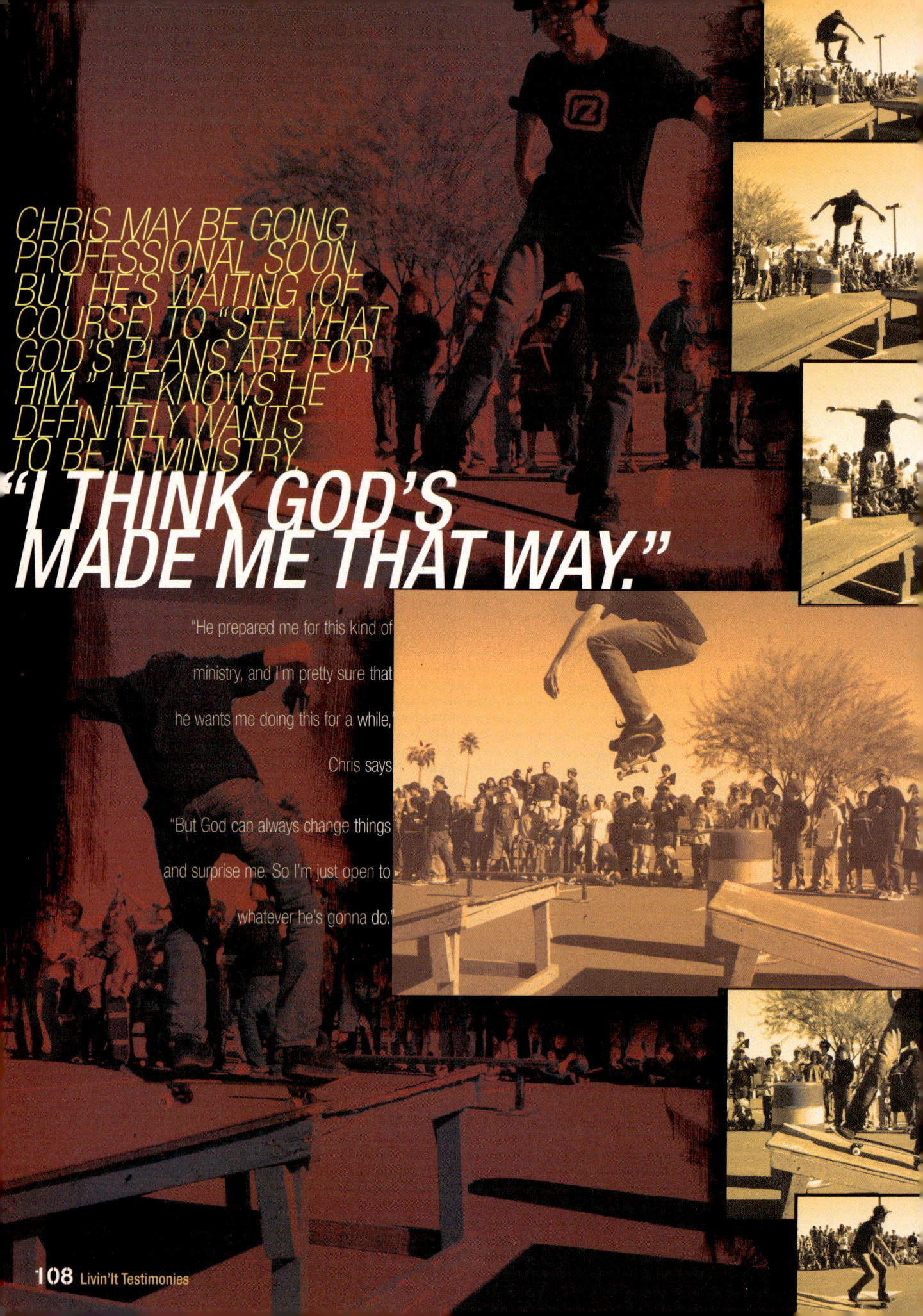

CHRIS MAY BE GOING PROFESSIONAL SOON. BUT HE'S WAITING (OF COURSE) TO "SEE WHAT GOD'S PLANS ARE FOR HIM." HE KNOWS HE DEFINITELY WANTS TO BE IN MINISTRY.

"I THINK GOD'S MADE ME THAT WAY."

"He prepared me for this kind of ministry, and I'm pretty sure that he wants me doing this for a while," Chris says. "But God can always change things and surprise me. So I'm just open to whatever he's gonna do."

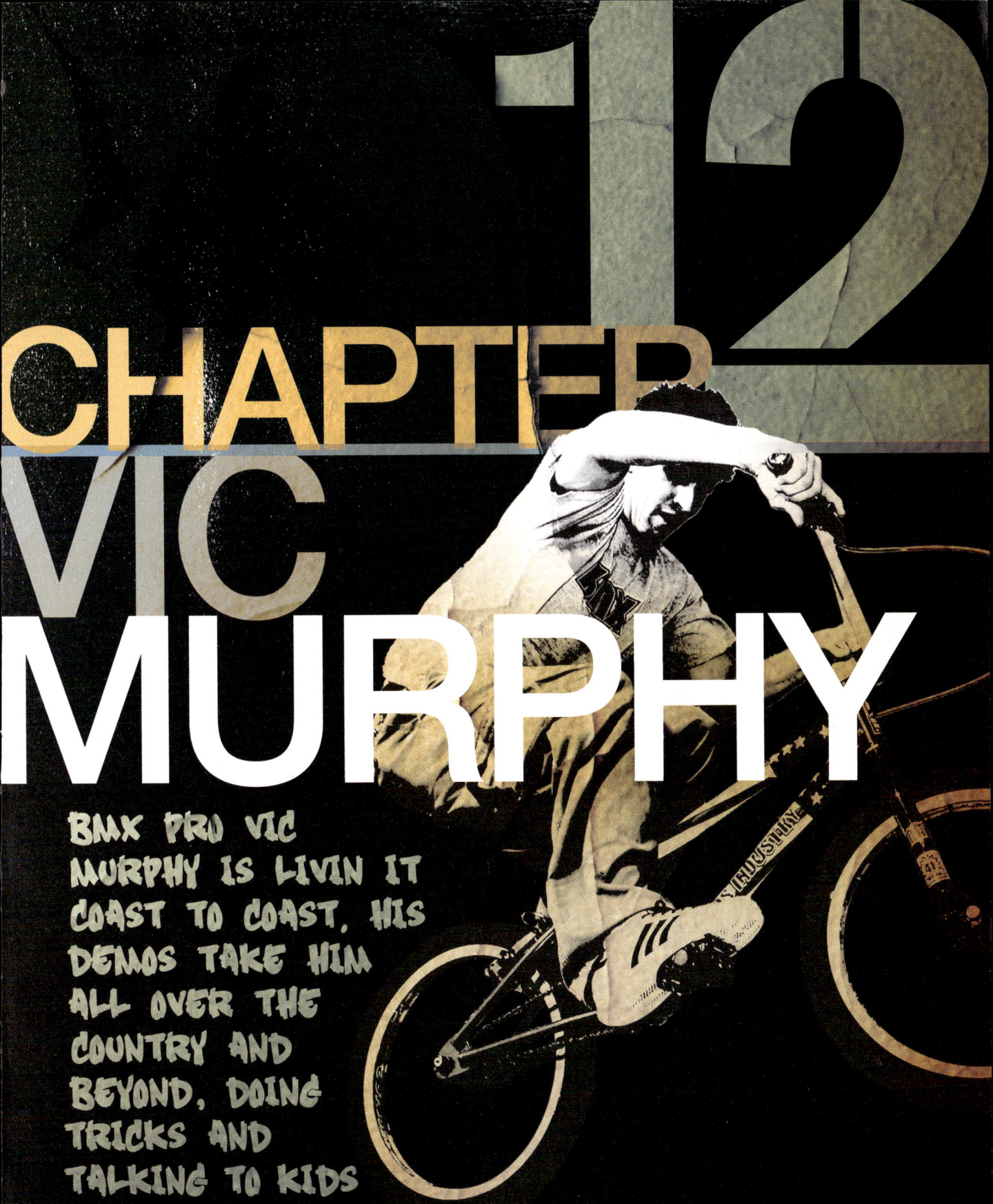

CHAPTER 12
VIC MURPHY

BMX PRO VIC MURPHY IS LIVIN IT COAST TO COAST, HIS DEMOS TAKE HIM ALL OVER THE COUNTRY AND BEYOND, DOING TRICKS AND TALKING TO KIDS

110 Livin'It Testimonies

Tossing his BMX magazine aside, Vic Murphy walked over to the window to check for the thousandth time. Still snowing. Snow, sleet, blizzard, an occasional avalanche, more snow. Kenai, Alaska, gets more than 60 inches of snow a year, and this year was no exception.

Since his parents' divorce four years earlier, twelve-year-old Vic had occupied much of his time with reading about BMX and getting out on his bike whenever he could. He lived for the day when the snow would finally melt, the streets would dry up, and he could once again take his bike out on the open road with his friends. But for now, one more turn around his dad's garage would have to do.

Fast-forward twenty-three years. Vic now lives in southern California, where he's a professional BMX bike rider and the owner of two successful companies.

But he doesn't just live for bike riding anymore.

HE'S GOT A NEW TAKE ON LIFE.

Of course, there were a few stops along the way.

By the time Vic was 16, he was really going places with his bike. Although he loved living in Alaska, it wasn't really a great place to kick off a career in BMX. (You think?) So when Vic had the opportunity to move to San Diego and live with his uncle, he jumped at the chance.

It didn't take long for him to fit right into the action sports culture of southern California. He started traveling around the country, entering contests like Meet the Street, interviewing for magazines, and winning his first pro contest at 17.

He turned pro that same year—and he's still at it today, almost 20 years later. He's seen a lot of changes over that time, especially in the general acceptance of extreme sports like BMX, skateboarding, snowboarding and surfing. Just having a book like the one you're reading—one that's all about guys who do this stuff—is pretty amazing, Vic says. "I mean, in the mid-80s

YOU COULDN'T GET PEOPLE TO EVEN GIVE YOU THE TIME OF DAY."

Vic Murphy 111

RADICAL *change*

INTERESTINGLY, THOUGH, one of the hot topics that was always talked about among the BMX riders Vic hung out with his whole life was "Who is God?" They enjoyed having philosophical discussions about the meaning of life and what God might have to do with it all.

When he was 21, Vic came across a book in a grocery store that caught his attention. It had something to do with God, and he thought if he read it, he could improve his arguments in the debates he had with his friends.

Vic never imagined, though, that buying that book would set him on a journey that would radically change his life.

The book talked about a man named Jesus, how he died for our sins, and how God loves us. "I saw that what I was missing in my life was God and living for Him," Vic remembers. "So I asked God to forgive me, and I told Him I wanted to live for Him. He blessed that prayer, and ever since that point I've lived my life for Jesus."

Giving his life over to the Lord reminded Vic of being eight years old, having his

ACTION SPORTS OUTREACH

Vic is taking his faith on the road with the Action Sports Outreach. Doing demonstrations at various churches and other events keeps Vic's skills on his bike sharp and gives him the chance to talk to kids about his faith in God.

He tells his audiences that living an "extreme life" for Jesus Christ definitely doesn't mean you have to give up doing extreme sports. Instead, "we encourage kids that whatever it is that God has given them, a talent or something they enjoy doing, they can use that to reach their friends."

With the Action Sports Outreach taking off, Vic is more excited than ever about being in BMX ministry. "My goal is just to be more and more dedicated to it as a full-time ministry, to organize more riders to make it a stronger tool, to encourage the athletes, and just to grow the whole ministry to be a strong influence and use it more and more to reach this generation."

For more information, check out www.actionsportsoutreach.com

grandmother lead him in a prayer. It was just a vague memory. But he'd never had anyone to follow up with him on that, to help him understand what it meant to be a follower of Jesus. So he had strayed away from God.

Even though he had screwed up a few times, Vic understood that he didn't need to be perfect to accept Jesus Christ. He says, "Jesus doesn't say to clean up first and then come to me. He just says, 'Come to me no matter where you're at and I'll forgive you and I'll love you.'"

So Vic came to him right where he was. And discovered that his life now had hope. "Once I asked God to be the Lord of my life and he forgave me, I had a purpose in my life—to share that love and that forgiveness with other people," he says.

Having a personal relationship with Christ gave Vic what he had been missing for 21 years. "Growing up I had a dream and desire to be a pro bike rider, and my dream came true. I got to be on the cover of magazines. I've been in videos. I'm world famous for bike riding.

"Yet before I knew Jesus I was empty and I had no hope. It wasn't filling me inside. I didn't have any hope or reason for life."

extreme Life

Today, Vic is not just about extreme sports—he's about extreme Life! "I ride now for outreach," he says. Besides being a full-time pastor at his church, Horizon Christian Fellowship, you can often find Vic traveling all over the country with different evangelistic associations, ready to talk about how God has changed his life.

"All the action sports ministries are growing, and I'm excited about it," Vic says. "But I believe God has raised me up to encourage the other athletes to use this as a tool to reach this generation of kids."

At the festivals and other outreach events, Vic and his friends—both BMXers and skateboarders—spend time doing tricks and talking with kids about action sports. But they also spend time talking about something that's important to each one of them—how to have a relationship with Jesus Christ.

At a recent demo at a giant church in Albuquerque, a 16-year-old boy showed up to watch the motocross trial demonstration and skateboarding and BMX tricks. After the demonstration, several of the pros shared their testimonies about becoming a Christian, and this guy came forward.

Vic remembers how amazed he was to see this 16-year-old come to the front all by himself. "He was crying and said, 'I don't want to play around anymore. I want to give my life to Jesus.' It was just so cool to see a kid by himself being bold, standing and just receiving the encouragement that we were giving and saying, 'Yeah, I want to live for Jesus.'

"It happens all the time."

Complete Forgiveness

Vic sees a lot of people who want to accept Christ but feel like they've done too many bad things and have lived a horrible life. That's when he loves to tell one of his favorite stories, from the Gospel of Luke, chapter 23:

"When Jesus was crucified, there were two thieves crucified on either side of him. One of the criminals was mocking Jesus and said, 'If you're God, why don't you get yourself off this cross?' The reason Jesus didn't, of course, is because he took the punishment that we deserve for our sins upon himself.

Livin'It Testimonies

"The crowds around were mocking Jesus and spitting on him, after he had been beaten and nailed on the cross. But Jesus, as he hung there, said, 'Forgive them, Father, for they don't know what they're doing.' One of the thieves saw the people mocking Jesus, and saw how he forgave them rather than getting mad, and he asked Jesus to forgive him for the life he had led.

"Romans 10:9 says that if you confess with your mouth that Jesus is Lord and believe in your heart that God raised Him from the dead, you will be saved. The thief on the cross did that," Vic explains. "He looked at Jesus and he said, 'You know what? This man doesn't deserve death on the cross, but I do.' And the first thing he did was to confess with his mouth that he was a sinner, and to confess that Jesus is Lord.

"The thief asked Jesus to remember him when he came into his kingdom. He believed that God was going to raise him from the dead. Jesus turned to him as that guy was dying—in the last moments of his life—and said 'Today you will be with me in paradise.'

"And it's that easy," Vic says. "It isn't about getting ourselves cleaned up and getting our suits on and going to church. It's about looking to Jesus and saying, 'I deserve the punishment for my sin,' and just believing in your heart that God raised Him from the dead.

"That's how much love Jesus has for us. He's not looking for what we can do for him. He's looking to save us from our sins. Satan had that thief on the cross and was going to bring him into hell that day, but Jesus continued to love him . . . and saved him."

VIC'S STATS

Birthday:
July 11, 1970

Height:
5'10"

Weight:
145 lbs.

Wife:
Shelly

Parents:
Tom and Sherry

Sister:
Kimberly

Hometown:
Kenai, Alaska

Favorite food:
Carne asada burritos

Favorite music:
worship music

Favorite Scripture:
Romans 8

Favorite trick:
table top

Injuries:
couple of broken ribs
broken wrist
front teeth knocked out

Sponsors:
Dan's Comp Bicycle Mail Order
Dirt Bros.
Industry Bicycle Hardware

116 Livin'It Testimonies

Vic Murphy 117

LIVIN IT

SO HOW DOES IT FEEL TO BE A PRO BIKE RIDER FOR NEARLY TWO DECADES, WIN CONTESTS, HAVE YOUR PICTURE ON THE COVERS OF MAGAZINES, AND BE INVOLVED IN VIDEOS LIKE THE LIVIN IT DVD WITH HOLLYWOOD ACTOR STEPHEN BALDWIN?

SURE, THAT'S ALL PRETTY COOL. BUT VIC ADMITS, "NOTHING COMPARES TO THE RELATIONSHIP I HAVE WITH JESUS. THERE'S NOTHING THAT COMES EVEN REMOTELY CLOSE TO HOW AWESOME IT IS TO KNOW GOD AND TO HAVE A RELATIONSHIP WITH HIM, TO BE USED BY HIM AND JUST TO BE ABLE TO SHARE HIS LOVE WITH OTHER PEOPLE. ANY TRICK YOU COULD POSSIBLY DO IN THIS WORLD WILL NOT COMPARE WITH THE LOVE GOD HAS FOR US AND HOW AWESOME IT IS TO BE ABLE TO LIVE YOUR LIFE FOR HIM."

VIC'S ADVICE TO OTHER CHRISTIAN BMXERS? "IN THE BOOK OF JAMES IN THE BIBLE, IT SAYS TO BE 'DOERS' OF THE WORD, NOT ONLY 'HEARERS.' THAT MEANS WE'VE GOT TO STOP MESSING AROUND . . . AND START LIVIN IT!"

MURPHY

Livin'It Testimonies

CHAPTER 13
BRAD COLEMAN

HE HASN'T EVEN GRADUATED HIGH SCHOOL YET, BUT BRAD COLEMAN HAS ALREADY MADE HIS ON-SCREEN APPEARANCE SKATEBOARDING IN TWO DIFFERENT FILMS. FIND OUT HOW THIS YOUNG ATHLETE MADE HIS WAY

Brad looks around

as he coasts over to the table to sign in. Wow, this is so cool, he thinks to himself as he steps on the end of his skateboard to flip it up, catching it with one hand. These guys look really good!

A guy with a clipboard and pen approaches. "Hey you!" he says, pointing at Brad. "You could be Stacy! We still need a double for him. How old are you?"

"I'm 15," Brad replies.

"Oh, you're too young," he says. "Well, let me get your name and number just in case." Brad gives him the information, then moves on to talk to some of the other guys.

Brad Coleman and his friend Andrew had come out for an open casting call for extras in the new Lords of Dogtown movie. Even though Brad didn't really expect anything to come of it, they decided it would be fun to try it out.

Two days later, though, Brad was sitting in class when he was called to the front office. His mom was there, and she immediately said, "The director needs you up there right now!" Brad had landed a role as a stunt double for Stacy Peralta, one of the three aspiring young skateboarders in the Dogtown remake. In fact, he and Andrew both ended up getting to do some tricks in the movie.

So not only did Brad get to miss the entire second semester of school— (pretty cool!)—but he also got to meet some famous skateboarders on the set. "I really looked up to those guys, and it was just one of those big moments for me," he says.

"My favorite skater of all time is Jay Adams. I'd never seen him before, so when I saw him [at the premier], I went up to him to shake his hand, and I just couldn't think of what to say. I was just, like, 'I'm Brad,' and I shook his hand, and he looked at me like I was some crazy guy. I was, like, shaking afterwards."

MOVIE MADNESS

It was actually Dogtown and Z-Boys (the documentary film that Lords of Dogtown was based on) that got Brad and his friends interested in skateboarding in the first place. After they watched it, they were inspired to go out and try some of the stuff they saw in the movie. Getting to be part of the Hollywood remake was totally a dream come true for Brad.

But his rise to stardom didn't stop there. The next year, he got to be part of the Livin It LA DVD, produced by Hollywood actor Stephen Baldwin.

"Actually, my grandma got me involved in Livin It," Brad says. "Stephen went and spoke at my grandma's church, the Crystal Cathedral, and afterwards she was waiting in line to get an autograph for me because she knew that I skateboarded."

When Brad's grandma mentioned to Stephen that her grandson was a skateboarder and was a stunt double in the Lords of Dogtown movie, Stephen asked if Brad was a Christian. She said "yes," and Stephen got Brad's number so he could give him a call.

Being part of Livin It LA gave Brad the chance to meet even skateboarders like Lance Mountain and Christian Hosoi. "My friends and I always saw him in magazines," Brad says about Christian. "We would look at his pictures and we just thought, 'He is so good.' It was really kind of like a trip just to be skating with someone like that."

So will Brad be appearing in any more Hollywood films? Maybe. He's had a blast so far doing the filming for these two, and he's definitely open to the idea.

"ACTUALLY, MY GRANDMA GOT ME INVOLVED, IN LIVIN IT"

BLASTING FOR THE

CHRISTIANITY HAS ALWAYS BEEN A PART OF BRAD'S LIFE.

His parents were Christians, so he grew up going to church, drawing pictures of Jesus, and singing all the songs. But he didn't really start to grasp the idea of what it meant to be a Christian until he was in the sixth grade. That's when he was baptized.

Today Brad is really discovering what it means to be living life for Jesus Christ. He knows that God was the one who allowed everything to work out so that he could be part of Lords of Dogtown and Livin It LA.

Plus, it's given him some opportunities to talk about his personal relationship with Jesus Christ. "I was actually driving to go skate with one of my buddies. We were in the car, I was sitting there, and we just started talking about life. He was saying, 'Yeah, I believe in, like, a bigger being and stuff,' but he just really didn't understand it, so I started talking to him about God and Jesus."

This friend of his was about to start a family, and he wanted to raise his kids right. So he was really open to talking with Brad about what the Bible had to say. He told Brad he was going to do it—go home and start reading the Bible. "It was cool that I could share that with him," Brad says, "because I never thought that he was the type of guy who would be open to learning about Jesus. But he was."

LORD

Brad Coleman

LORDS OF DOGTOWN

Lords of Dogtown takes the documentary film *Dogtown and Z-Boys* and gives it a Hollywood twist. It's set in the '70s skate culture of Venice, California (a.k.a. Dogtown) and follows the story of three surfers-turned-skateboarders: Stacy, Jay, and Tony.

Written by Stacy Peralta and based on his own life, the film highlights the rise of skateboarding as a popular sport. The legendary Z-boys took the daring moves of surfing and applied them to skateboarding, making themselves into overnight sensations and transforming the skateboard industry—as well as the youth culture—of southern California and beyond!

BRAD'S STATS

Birthday:
November 13, 1988

Height:
5'9"

Weight:
140 lbs.

Parents:
Ann and T.R.

Brother:
Zach

Hometown:
Lake Forest, California

Favorite food:
Italian

Favorite music:
classic rock

Favorite Bible verses:
John 3:16 –
"It's the first verse
I ever remember learning"

Favorite Trick:
Indy nosebone

Career high:
being a stunt double in the
Lords of Dogtown movie

Career High: **BEING A STUNT DOUBLE IN THE LORDS OF DOGTOWN MOVIE**

FAVORITE BIBLE VERSES: **JOHN 3:16**

Brad Coleman 125

"*At the skatepark* where Brad works now, he and a friend have started a Thursday night Bible study. They skate for a while with their friends, and then each week they alternate doing a short lesson about something from God's Word. Now in his final year of high school, Brad is looking forward to going to college. He's also considering going into firefighting. Or you might see him appear in another movie. He's just waiting to see what God has for him next.

WAIT TO SEE WHAT GOD HAS FOR YOU NEXT

CHAPTER 14
LUKE BRADOCK

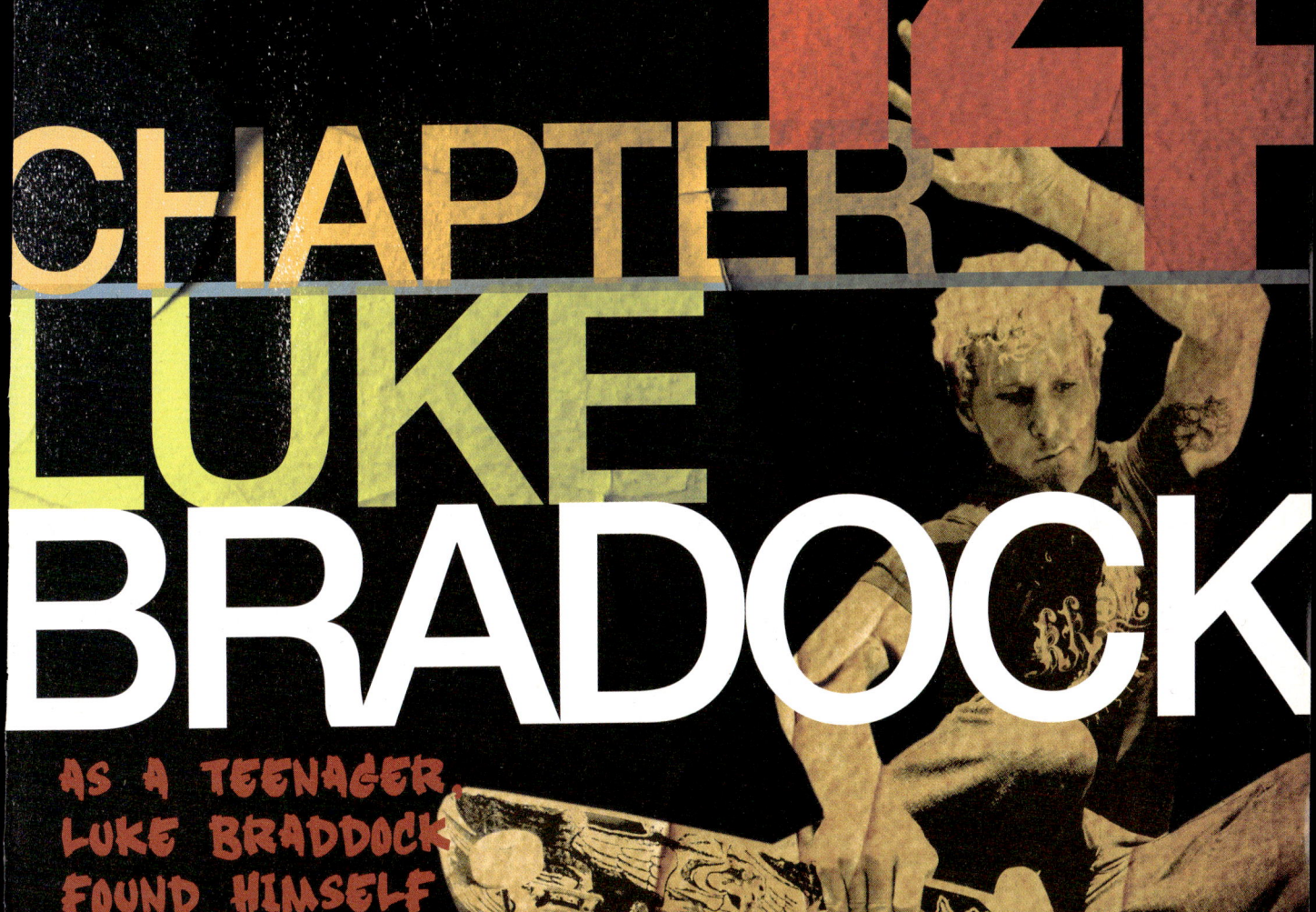

As a teenager, Luke Braddock found himself struggling to fit in with the cool crowd. Skateboarding offered him recognition and success, but it wasn't until he handed over control of his life that he found true happiness.

SEARCHING

AS A TEENAGER,
Luke wanted what every kid wants—to fit in. But in his attempt to earn credibility with his friends and be considered cool, he went through a rebellious period, turning to skateboarding, partying, and bad relationships to fill the void he felt.

When he was seven, he had prayed with his mother and accepted Christ into his heart, but he wasn't living like a Christian anymore.

"My parents are strong Christians and super solid, but they forced me to go to church, and it kinda turned me away from it a little bit. I had to go out on my own and live life and get beat up before I realized that I couldn't depend on my own self. I didn't realize my identity was in Christ."

During his junior year of high school, Luke joined a youth outreach program called Young Life. "The leaders at Young Life were sharing God's love with me. It reminded me again what my life should be like."

Basically, Luke found himself at a point where he was empty and unsatisfied, and he realized he needed God to change his life because he was sick of the way he was living.

4 MEANING

At a Young Life camp, Luke rededicated his life to Jesus Christ. "And ever since, God's been developing me into the man he wants me to be. I know he has big plans, and I'm just trying to stay true to him so that he can reveal those plans to me and I won't miss out on the opportunity."

From that point on, Luke was ready to live for God. "As soon as God changed my heart, I learned that my skateboarding could be used as a tool to draw kids closer to God. I learned that I could use a piece of wood and rubber wheels to initiate conversations with kids and give them the chance to get the gospel."

After working at Young Life as a leader, Luke spent a few years in college. He then got involved with King of Kings Skateboard Ministry, where he was able to talk about his relationship with God while getting to ride his board a lot.

"God has done so many things with my life and with skateboarding," he says. "It's been amazing. I've gone places I never thought I'd go. I've seen things I never thought I would see. I've met the raddest people.

"God didn't put us on this earth so we could just live and die, but so we can live and have a personal relationship with him and experience life to the fullest."

Luke Braddock **129**

LUKE'S STATS

Birthday:
October 30, 1981

Height:
5'8"

Weight:
155 lbs.

Wife:
Tonyisha

Parents:
Cindy and Dave

Siblings:
Heath, Joel and Hanna

Hometown:
Prunedale, California

Favorite food:
Authentic Mexican

Favorite music:
Rock n' Roll

Favorite Bible verses:
Proverbs 3:5-6
Jeremiah 29:11

Favorite trick:
Miller flip

Major Injuries:
Ruptured spleen
a few concussions
two broken wrists
front teeth broken out

Sponsors:
Reliance Skateboards
King of Kings Skateboard Ministry
Vans Shoes
Krux Trucks
Sessions Clothing
Ninja Bearings
Bill's Wheels Skate Shop

Luke Braddock **131**

LIVIN IT ALL-OUT
4 God

Living life to the fullest is exactly what Luke is doing now—and he's seeing some amazing results. After one demonstration, a young kid came up to him and said, "You're cooler than Tony Hawk."

"I knew I wasn't as good a skateboarder as Tony Hawk," Luke explains, "But the connection that kid had with me was that I was offering him the love of God. He thought I was cool because I had something else, and he thought that was rad."

Luke knows he can feel good when young kids look up to him, because through Christ he is able to set a godly example. "I remember when I was a kid, I was looking for that same thing—someone just to stand up and do the right thing—and now I'm able to do that and lead by example," he says.

Of course, Luke will quickly admit that it can be nerve-racking to stand up in front of thousands of people and talk about God. But as he shares what's on his heart and sees kids come forward—crying and wanting to receive Jesus Christ as their Savior—he knows it's worth it.

What's the secret message that brings teenage guys to tears?

WAITING FOR THE ONE

When Luke first met Tonyisha, they were both leaders in the Young Life youth ministry program. "She worked with the junior high group and I worked in the high school, but I taught her how to snowboard at one of our camps," Luke says. "We just started hanging out and discovered that we were meant to be together."

Luke and Tonyisha dated for 2½ years while they were in college, and then had a nine month engagement before they were married in August 2005. Through that whole time they made a commitment to each other and to God that they would not have sex until they were married.

"Our friends were pretty surprised," Luke admits, "A few people found out and they would tell everybody, and they're like, 'What? These guys are virgins?!'"

Keeping their commitment to save sex for marriage was certainly not the easiest choice, but Luke and Tonyisha know it was the right one. They understood that sex outside of marriage has caused all kinds of damage, both physical (AIDS and other STDs) and emotional (divorce, hurt, anger, broken relationships).

"Sure, sex is great. After all, God created it! But he created it to happen within the special, intimate bond of marriage." Luke and Tonyisha have discovered that honoring God brings them more joy and fulfillment than anything else.

It's actually really simple, Luke says. "I basically just tell them that Christ wants to have a personal relationship with you. He wants you to live life to the fullest. The only way you can receive this is by admitting you've sinned and that you need him to save you.

"He's not going to force himself upon you. He gave us a free will, and we have to choose to love him. Otherwise he would have created us as robots, and he would have been like, 'You gotta love me.' But he didn't do it that way. It's our choice to either obey him or listen to our own selfish desires and do what we want."

Luke Braddock

Luke chose to accept
GOD'S FREE OFFER OF SALVATION
through Jesus Christ,

and he hasn't regretted it. "I definitely went through times that were difficult even though I was following Christ, but those difficult times have just developed character in my life and perseverance and the faith that I now have
IN JESUS CHRIST AS MY LORD AND SAVIOR.

Luke Braddock 135

"I'VE DONE A LOT OF THINGS AND SEEN A LOT OF THINGS AND TRIED A LOT OF THINGS, **BUT NOTHING COMPARES TO THE GOODNESS OF GOD** *AND KNOWING THAT YOU'RE IN HIS WILL. THAT'S JUST REAL, THAT'S WHERE IT'S AT."*

Now he's just "taking it one day at a time. The Christian life isn't always easy, but it's always fulfilling. Being on the road and touring with King of Kings is what God has for him right now, and Luke plans to keep doing it as long as God wants him there.

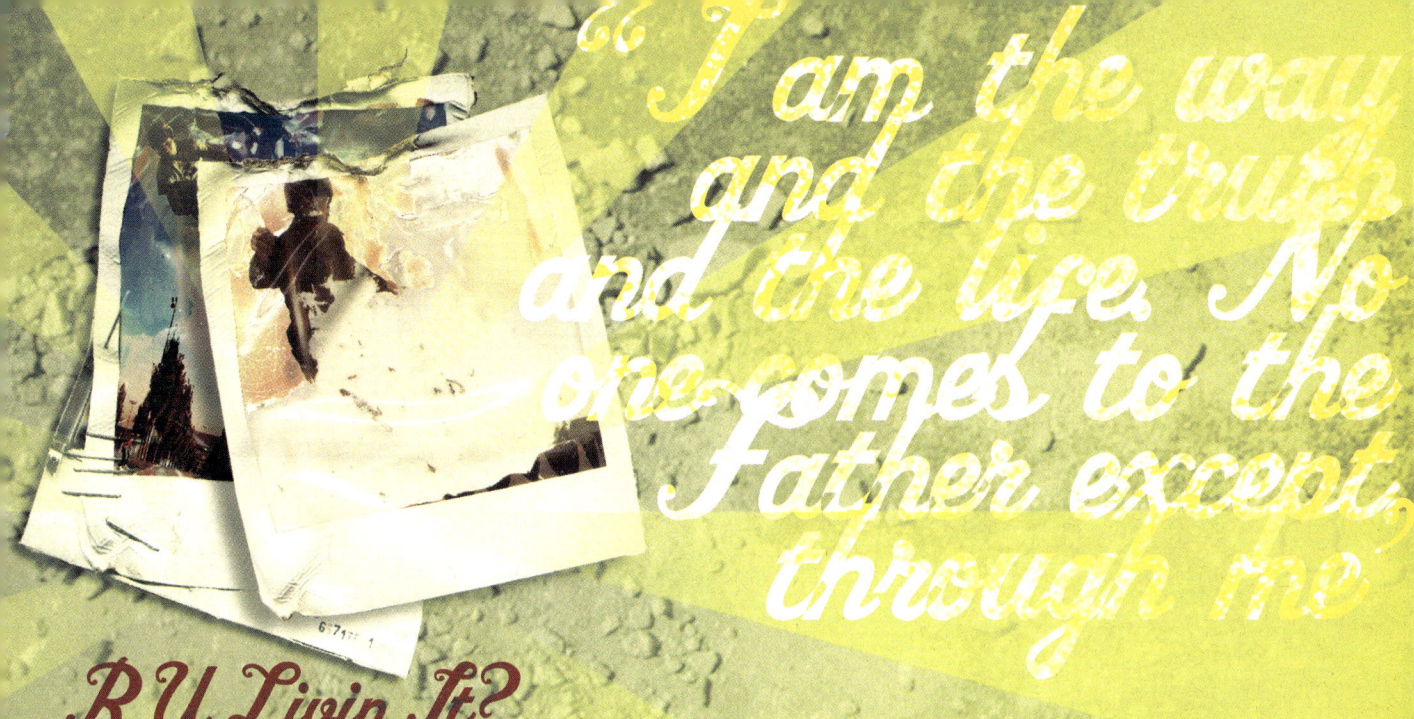

"I am the way and the truth and the life. No one comes to the Father except through me."

R U Livin It?

The Bible says that God created you and actually wants to have a relationship with you. He wants you to live forever with him. When Jesus came to the world, he said, "I came that people might have life and have it to the full" (John 10:10).

So if God wants you to know him, why don't you? Well, there's a problem, and it's called sin.

Our sin separates us from God.

The Bible says that "All have sinned; all fall short of God's glorious standard" (Romans 3:23 NLT). That means every person who's ever lived has done bad things. (That's what sin is—bad things.) And God has to punish those things. Just like a judge on earth wouldn't let you do something wrong and then just let you go, God isn't either. The Bible actually says, "The wages of sin is death" (Romans 6:23).

But the cool thing about it is, "death" isn't our only option in life. The last part of that same verse says, "The [free] gift of God is eternal life in Christ Jesus our Lord." Instead of sending us to die and then go to hell forever (which is where people are punished for their sins) . . .

Jesus Christ actually paid the penalty for our sins.

Jesus was treated as if he lived your sinful life, so that God could treat you as if you had lived Jesus' perfect life. So do you want to die as an unforgiven sinner? Or do you want to let Jesus, who already died in your place on the cross, take away your sins?

When Jesus was alive he said, "I am the way and the truth and the life. No one comes to the Father except through me" (John 14:6). There's no other way you can get your sins forgiven. So that's what you need to do if you want to accept his forgiveness.

You need to admit you're a sinner.

You can't just go, "That's cool" and not really take it to heart. But if you're thinking, 'Lord, my sins killed you, and I'm sorry, and I don't want to treat you like that anymore. I don't want to live my life that way"—that's called repenting. And God forgives everyone who repents.

You need to believe.

If that's where you're at—if you believe that Jesus lived and died and rose for you, and you believe that he can forgive you, and you're ready to say you're sorry and turn from your sins and give him the leadership of your life, then you're ready to receive him.

If you would like to become a Christian right now, you can pray this prayer to God, or you can use your own words to tell him how you feel.

Father in heaven, I believe that you sent your Son Jesus to forgive my sins. I know I've done a lot of bad things in my life. I'm sorry. I turn away from those sins, Jesus. I don't want to do them anymore. I want you to come into my heart and forgive me, to lead my life the way it should have been lived in the first place. Thank you, Jesus, for dying for me, for rising from the dead, for being alive, and for coming into my life. And thank you that I'm now your child. I want to live for you forever. In Jesus' name, Amen.

If you prayed that and meant it, you're one of our brothers. You're now a child of God and you can start livin it! All of us who are a part of Livin It would be stoked to hear that you have given your life to the Lord. Write to us and let us know!

ACKNOWLEDGMENTS

Many, many people worked together to bring you Livin It: Testimonies. Special thanks go to…

…The entire Livin It team for their commitment to seeing this book published. Rick Weigele, Maile Weigele, Kevin Palau, David Jones, Katie Bredemeier, Heidi Cox, Dave Redelfs, Monica Oliver, Kirk Purdy, and Stephanie Newman, thank you for everything!

…Elizabeth Jones and David Sanford for conducting the interviews and drafting the chapters, Rebekah Clark for reviewing the manuscript, and the rest of the team at Sanford Communications, Inc., for their assistance and guidance. Also, to Karen Weitzel for transcribing all the interviews.

…Mike Ross at Breakaway Magazine for seeing the potential in the stories of the some of the athletes featured in this book.

…Lawrence Kimbrough, Jeff Godby, Roy Roper (wideyedesign), Blake Morgan and the entire Broadman & Holman family for their tireless work on the cover and interior designs.

Of course, this book would not have been possible without the super guys who have shared their stories with you: Anthony Carney, Brad Coleman, Bruce Crisman, Chris Weigele, Christian Hosoi, Elijah Moore, Jared Lee, Jeremiah Anderson, Josh Kasper, Luke Braddock, Phil Trotter, Sierra Fellers, Tim Bryne, and Vic Murphy.

Tim Byrne photos courtesy of Spirit Media. Jeremiah Anderson photos courtesy of Jennifer Anderson. Anthony Carney photos courtesy of Huey Huynh. Vic Murphy photos courtesy of Scott Papiro. Brad Coleman photos on pages 119, 122, and 125 Courtesy of Eric "Arab" Groff. All others courtesy Luis Palau Association.